In the Valley of
the Little Big Horn

June 25-26, 1876

In the Valley of the Little Big Horn

The 7th and the Sioux

ROBERT C. KAIN

Beinfeld Publishing Inc.
North Hollywood, California

Copyright © 1969 by Robert C. Kain, 2nd edition copyright © December 1975. All rights reserved. No portion of this book may be reproduced, copied, or duplicated by any means or by any system, including data storage or tape recording, without prior written consent. Brief exceprts for the purpose of review only are permitted.

Published by Beinfeld Publishing, Inc., North Hollywood, California

Library of Congress Cataloging in Publication Data

Kain, Robert C.
In the Valley of the Little Big Horn.

Reprint of the ed. published by the author, Newfane, Vt.
1. Little Big Horn, Battle of the, 1876.
2. Custer, George Armstrong, 1839-1876.
3. United States. Army. 7th Cavalry. I. Title.
[E83.876.K3 1978]   973.82   78-16021
ISBN 0-917714-16-4

Beinfeld Publishing, Inc. edition 1st printing, July 1978

DEDICATION

To the memory of the forgotten men of the
Little Big Horn

CONTENTS

		Page
	Author's Foreword —	ix
	Colonel's Military Biography	xi
	Preface	xvii
1	A Look to the West, 1862-74	1
2	The Long Trail	13
3	Major Reno's Charge	33
4	The Reunion	49
5	Stand of the Combined Command	65
6	Custer's Last Mile	77
7	The Forgotten Men of the Little Big Horn	93

AUTHOR'S FOREWORD

This is a new printing of, "In the Valley of the Little Big Horn," first published in 1969. Though this cannot be called a revised edition, as historical fact brooks no revision, this volume has been enhanced by the addition of personal notes and comments by the late Colonel Edward M. Offley, United States Cavalry, retired. His notes have been reproduced here, just as he wrote them, on the page margins, in his own hand.

In the late summer of 1970, after having read a copy of the first edition of my book, the Colonel wrote to me and very graciously offered to annotate a copy that I might keep. He expressed his deep interest in the subject and explained how it had touched his life.

Though the Colonel was not born until two years after the battle, he relates that he often heard the engagement discussed in detail by members of the Offley family, who were in the military forces that participated in the Indian campaigns of that era. He, himself, served as a cavalry trooper at the turn of the century where he rode with men who had fought in the valley of the Little Big Horn. In his own words, he writes in reference to the battle, "I heard it described and discussed many times around camp fires, in the field, and in officer's mess by actual participants."

In spite of the fact that the Colonel was ninety two years old at the time he wrote the comments contained in this book, he was blessed with a steady hand, clear mind, and unfailing memory. I say, "was," because Colonel Offley passed away suddenly, in the fall of 1970, within a day of completing the thoughts he recorded for us here.

We came alarmingly close to missing the opportunity of preserving one more of the precious threads that helps to tie the gossamer fabric of our past, to the pattern of our present day realities. His life lacked but a few short years of spanning the entire second century of our nation's existence. He did actually live, what most of us can only refer to, as history.

The next few pages are a short autobiographical description of the military career of Colonel Edward M. Offley — Cavalry Trroper, Officer, Gentleman.

Robert C. Kain
July, 1978

Comments by Colonel Edward M. Offley, Cavalry, U.S. Army, Retired, on the book entitled "In the Valley of the Little Big Horn", by Robert C. Kain, RFD, Newfane, Vermont, 05345.

This is a well written and, in my opinion, a brief but essentially complete and accurate account of the part played in the campaign against the Sioux and Cheyenne Indians in 1876 by the 7th U.S. Cavalry under the command of Lieutenant Colonel, (Brevet Major General), George Armstrong Custer, U.S. Army. In addition to these remarks, I have made many marginal notes in the copy of the book loaned me by Mrs. Francis Mallory, Fairfax, Virginia.

In my early boyhood I have heard my father and some of his old Army friends discuss the part played by George Armstrong Custer in the Little Big Horn campaign which awakened an interest in the subject which remains with me to the present day. The interest of my father, Holmes Edward Offley, stemmed from the fact that he had an older brother, Lieutenant Colonel Robert Hilton Offley, 17th Infantry, who was stationed at Fort Abraham Lincoln, Dakota Territory, at the same time that Custer and the 7th Cavalry were stationed there and, further, that he had a young nephew and name-sake, Holmes Offley Paulding, Assistant Surgeon, U.S. Army, also stationed there and attached to the 7th Cavalry, — see his picture on page 4 of the book.

I have heard and read much on the subject, but what has made it so real to me is the fact that I have personally known and served with a number of those officers and men who took part in that campaign, some of whom were with Custer up to the last hour or two of his life. Between the end of the year of 1898 and the middle of 1901, I served in the old Regular Army as Private, Corporal, Sergeant and 1st Sergeant of Troop G, 1st U.S. Cavalry, being stationed at old Fort Meade in the Black Hills and Sioux country of South Dakota and Fort Yellowstone, Wyoming. Many of the officers and a few of the enlisted men with whom I served had seen service in many fights with the Sioux, the Cheyennes, the Nez Percés and other tribes and a considerable number of them in the Little Big Horn Campaign.

In the summer of 1900 my troop was ordered to change station from Fort Meade, South Dakota, to Fort Yellowstone, Wyoming. On the way to our new station we passed the Custer battlefield and I remember vividly the little white markers scattered all over the hill where Custer made his last stand, each marking the grave of one of the officers or men who went to their deaths with Custer and a few days later were buried, each of them just where they had fallen. Since then, as I understand it, their remains have been gathered together and re-interred in a small, fenced in cemetery now classed as a National Historic Monument, but I believe permanent markers were placed to show where each fell.

At the time of my enlisted service and for some time later our uniforms, arms, (carbine, pistol and sabre) and both personal and horse equipment were practically identical with those used in 1876 and earlier. In fact, practically all of the sabres in the troop were stamped with dates showing that they had been made during or before the Civil War or earlier. The carbines, however, were of an improved model. The full-dress uniform I wore on ceremonial occasions was the same as those of the officers pictures on 101-105, except that mine lacked the shoulder knots of an officer, (added later when I received my commission), instead of which I wore on each sleeve the large, yellow chevron, pointed down, with the lozenge, (diamond shaped), of a 1st Sergeant, and also except the flowing yellow horsehair plume atop my helmet and the breast cords with tassle looped across from shoulder to shoulder were not of quite as fine quality as those of an officer.

In 1901, I received my commission as 2nd Lieutenant of Cavalry, a beautifully engraved piece of parchment, signed personally, as was then the custom, by the President of the United States, the Secretary of War and The Adjutant General of the Army. What a proud day that was in my life! I was assigned to the 12th U.S. Cavalry, a new regiment then being organized at Fort Sam Houston, Texas. In a short time I had my troop, F, 12th Cavalry, organized, supplied, equipped, mounted and fairly well trained, and was ordered to proceed in command of it, (though only a brand new, "shave-tail" 2nd Lieutenant), to Fort Clark, an old Mexican border post about 130 miles west of San Antonio. When the regiment was fully organized, the Colonel, Whelan; the Lieutenant Colonel, Edward S. Godfrey; two of the Majors, Luther R. Hare and Winfield Scott Edgerly; and the senior Captain, William J. Nicholdon, "Slicker Bill", had all served in the 7th Cavalry in the Little Big Horn campaign, (see mention of some of them throughout the book). As a result, the 12th Cavalry came, for a while, to be known as the "Junior Seventh". As soon as I could, I transferred from the 12th back to my old regiment, the 1st Cavalry and served in it until World War I, – over sixteen years as a lieutenant.

I will try to give my personal opinion of Custer and I hope I will be forgiven if I judge him unfairly. I don't think anyone can dispute his personal, individual bravery. At West Point he was frequently in trouble and barely scraped through, graduating just as the Civil War broke out. At the first Battle of Manassas, Lieutenant Custer's gallant conduct caught the eyes of some of his higher commanders, and still in his early twenties he was promoted to the rank of Brigadier General, to be followed, at what the Preface of the book calls the "tender age of 24", to that of Major General of Volunteers. He did some outstanding service during the "Peninsula Campaign" of 1862, and in the cavalry fight between the Union and Confederate cavalry, about two miles east of the main battle field of Gettysburg, July 3, 1863, Custer, commanding a brigade, deserves much credit for having played a part in saving the Union cavalry from being swept from the field in defeat. Later in that war, – serving under General Phil Sheridan in the Shenandoah Valley, – Custer won the hatred and contempt of the inhabitants of that part of Virginia, which was still very much in evidence during my school days there. In order to put a stop to Lee's army being supplied from that region, it was decided to destroy that source of supply. Custer, under command of Phil Sheridan, proceeded to lay waste the area, – burning every barn, the crops, killing the live stock from cattle to chickens and, in many cases destroying the homes occupied by old men, women and children. When that Custer "victory" was all over, it is asserted that Sheridan boasted that "a crow flying over the Shenandoah Valley would have to carry his rations with him!"

The 7th Cavalry was organized in 1866 and was still a very new regiment in 1876. Custer, having returned to his Regular Army rank of Lieutenant Colonel, was assigned to the command of it. How well trained it was in that short time, I would not presume to say. However, Custer had given it a certain kind of "Esprit de Corps", (in my opinion a very "phony" one), which it retained even after its defeat on the banks of the Little Big Horn, and up to my days as an officer in the 1st Cavalry, it was continually *boasting* of its defeat, which we of the older regiments never could understand. In fact, at about the same time as the Sioux-Cheyenne campaign, the 1st Cavalry, further west, was fighting the Nez Percés in Idaho and Montana and on one occasion, two troops of the 1st Cavalry were led up to a coulee into a blind canyon known as "White Bird Canyon" in Idaho, by Chief Joseph and were completely wiped out. Their bodies were recovered and buried at old Fort Walla Walla, Washington, where I was stationed with the 1st Cavalry later on. Whilst not ashamed of that incident, it was a regimental "family secret" of which we were not proud and certainly never boasted of it or even mentioned it outside of "the family", — the regiment.

It has long been my own private opinion of Custer that it was his lack of long years of service in the lower commissioned ranks and the experience that goes with it and teaches the "tricks of the trade" that made him so "cock-sure" of himself and unable to take the advice of his junior officers who were far superior to him as Indian fighters. His handling of his regiment on the Little Big Horn, dividing into four distantly separated parts, each out of supporting distance of the other, in the face of what he must have known was a *powerful,* if not *superior* force, violated all the principles of tactics which even a lowly corporal or sergeant was taught.

One more point and I am through. I could almost write a book on the subject, which I at one time considered doing, but the matter has been amply covered by more accomplished writers.

It was in connection with Custer's behaviour at the time of the Washita fight, (pages 7 and 8), where, instead of following Major Elliott and supporting him, he lingered all day, even showing off what a fine pistol shot he was by personally shooting many of the Indian's ponies, and even dogs, — that, and his cruel punishment of his men for slight breaches of discipline, — so turned some of his officers against him that they preferred charges as a result of which he was tried by a General Court Martial, found guilty and "suspended from rank, pay and command" for one year. In my opinion, it was a great pity that he was not there and then dismissed from the service, which might have saved his life and that of many others on the banks of the Little Big Horn.

The author of this book, Robert C. Kain, deserves much credit for tracing the names and origins of the enlisted men of Custer's command, the first time, I believe, it has been done. They gave their lives as a price for, what I consider to be, the stupidity of their glory-seeking commander.

Edward M. Coffey

Williamsburg, Virginia,
21 February 1970.

Colonel, Cavalry, U.S. Army,
Retired.

PREFACE

ON JUNE 25th and 26th, 1876, one of the worst defeats of the American Indian Wars was suffered by the 7th Regiment of U. S. Cavalry. Brevet Major General George Armstrong Custer, 253 of his troopers, 3 Indian scouts and 7 civilians were killed by hostile Sioux and Cheyenne Indians on the banks of the Little Big Horn River, Montana Territory.

Much is known and has been written of George Armstrong Custer, the golden haired boy wonder, who attained the rank of Major General during the Civil War at the tender age of 24. There has been a good deal of controversy over the years since his defeat and death in what has become known as "Custer's Last Stand". Some believe him to have been a blundering idiot, solely responsible for the tragic results of the battle. Others can envision him doing no wrong, and lay the blame for the staggering death toll during the two-day engagement on the shoulders of Major Marcus A. Reno, the Regiment's second in command.

The aim of this book is neither to condemn nor exonerate General Custer. It is, rather, the presentation of the facts concerning the battle in as much detail and truth as possible.

Almost everyone who has even briefly explored the story of the Little Big Horn is familiar with General Custer and his brothers, Tom and Boston. The names of Major Reno, Captains Benteen, Keogh, Yates; Lieutenants Porter, Harrington, McIntosh and Calhoun are mentioned in nearly every account of the action. Even Captain Keogh's horse, Comanche, has

In the Valley of the Little Big Horn

galloped out of the mists of the past, to be memorialized on the printed page and on the wide screen of our theatres. But who were the enlisted men who followed Custer into battle and stood at his side until death took them, one by one? Where did they come from? What cities, states, or countries did they call home? These men were as alive and real in their day as we are today in ours. They were all <u>fathers,</u> sons, or husbands, with families and friends.

We are used to seeing the U.S. Cavalry charge across our movie and T.V. screens, and in the heat of battle when a blue clad soldier is cut down, we know in the back of our minds that when the picture is over, the dead trooper will get up, dust his breeches, and go home to supper. But the troopers of the Little Big Horn never did rise. They were buried beneath the soil where they fell, and in the pages of history, as simply 264 men. Custer lives on in the legend of Custer's Last Stand, yet he did not stand and fall alone.

When I first began to research this subject, the identity of these men was my sole concern. I lay no claim to being an historian or author. I am a firearms engraver, and I am always most interested in employing a historical vehicle to carry my work. This small piece of Americana is ideally suited. My intention is to engrave 263 Colt Revolvers, Single Action Army 45, Model 1873, to represent these soldiers; to incise in lasting steel the name and other statistics of each man who lost his life at the Battle of the Little Big Horn.

In searching for the facts pertaining to the identity of the troopers, I was led into many books, always with the same frustrating results; a different story emerged each time. Nowhere could I find an accurately detailed list of the men who had died in the most written-about military engagement of the past one hundred years. After making many inquiries, I at last found refuge in the official Army records supplied at nominal cost by the National Archives, Washington, D. C. This information was on two rolls of 35 m.m. microfilm. I rigged it

xviii

Preface

in a borrowed slide projector, and with the help of my wife and some friends, we set about the eye straining task of searching the 95 year old records of thousands of U.S. Soldiers. It was like bringing a piece of the early days of the West into our living room. As our guests left after a session, the question was always the same, when shall we do this again? Everyone who helped search, and was rewarded by finding the forgotten name of a trooper who played such a dramatic part in our early American History, became as enthusiastic and sincerely interested, as my wife and I. It was not long before we had searched over six years of army records, and attained the elusive goal we sought; the identity and origin of the Forgotten Men of the Little Big Horn.

With the list now complete, there was still one piece of vital information lacking: the dispersement of troops as ordered by General Custer on the afternoon of June 25th. It was my desire to identify the individual command, as Custer, Reno, Benteen, or McDougall, that each trooper rode with on his last day.

I had been advised by the National Archives that this microfilm information was available in the records of the Court of Inquiry. Upon securing and studying the copies, I found that I had uncovered such a wealth of neglected, factual information about the engagement that I could not resist setting it down on paper.

Among the first few pages of the text of the Court of Inquiry appears the following special order:

> Headquarters of the Army
> Adjutant General's Office
> Washington, November 25, 1878

Special Orders
No. 255

By direction of the President and on the application of Major Marcus A. Reno, 7th Cavalry, a Court of Inquiry is hereby appointed to assemble at Chicago, Illinois on Monday the 13th day of January 1879, or as soon there-

In the Valley of the Little Big Horn

Maj. Marcus A. Reno

after as practical for the purpose of inquiring into Major Reno's conduct at the Battle of the Little Big Horn River on the 25th and 26th days of June, 1876.

The court will report the facts and its opinion as to whether from all the circumstances in the case, any further proceedings are necessary.

By the command of General Sherman
(Signed)
E. D. Townsend,
Adjutant General

Testimony was taken under oath from a total of 23 witnesses. Eleven were officers of the 7th Regiment who participated in the fighting. Three were enlisted men and five were civilian participants. There were also officers who visited the battleground later as observers.

The question of General Custer's responsibility for the disastrous defeat was not pertinent to the investigation of the court and was not discussed. What *was* being looked into by the court was the conduct of Major Reno during the action. He had been accused, by critics, of having caused the death of

Preface

Custer and his men by cowardice on his part. Major Reno suffered with these accusations for 2½ years, and finally requested a Court of Inquiry to investigate the charges and clear his slandered name. The investigation subsequently exonerated Major Reno of any misconduct or cowardice, and coincidentally exposed facts that gave a clear and accurate picture concerning events immediately preceding the battle.

My object here is to present the story of the battle as I found it in the testimony. As for responsibility for the tragedy, you may draw your own conclusions.

The reluctance of the government to release the facts concerning the Custer disaster promptly resulted in confusion and fabrication at the time; the effect of which may still be found today, more than 90 years later. If you read several accounts of the engagement, you find, though they will be basically the same, they will vary widely in important details and bristle with inaccuracies and inconsistencies. It is apparent that many books, articles, and even usually reliable authoritative sources of reference have unwittingly been infected by the propagation of these erroneous tales.

On the pages that follow is the complete and accurate story of the Battle of the Little Big Horn. The accounts of all action from the time the 7th Regiment left the Rosebud River have come directly from the minutes of the Court of Inquiry. The only liberty I have taken was to arrange the testimony of the witnesses in proper sequence, in an attempt to carry the reader through the encounter, as it occurred. I have injected explanatory phrases and descriptive adjectives to illustrate the battle as I saw it in my mind's eye, and to keep this account from becoming a dry recital of facts.

In order to fully appreciate the significance of this engagement, it is necessary to know something of the events that preceded. In the first chapter, I have attempted to sketch a clear picture of conditions that existed on the frontier in regard to hostile Indian activities between 1862 and the battle date of June 25, 1876.

xxi

CHAPTER 1

A Look to the West 1862-74

AS THE THUNDER of the Civil War died away to a diminishing rumble in April 1865, this young nation of thirty-six states began the task of mending the fractured union. Now that it had survived the crisis of near death in its infancy, it looked to the west, anxious to resume the interrupted growth that would bring it to its full potential in strength and size.

During the war, the major portion of both armies, north and south, had little time for anything but each other. Scant force was left from either side to hold the hostile Indians of the territories in check, and the boundary line of the western frontier was marked with blood from the Canadian border to Mexico. In Minnesota, Little Crow of the Santee Sioux led a short but violent uprising against the white inhabitants of that fledgling state in 1862, while in Texas, Mangas Coloradas and his Apaches rode the entire frontier in between, at will, pressing hard on the outposts of civilization. Throughout a large section of the border states and territories, where the paths of the north, south and hostiles crossed and recrossed, it was much like a three cornered free for all, each striking the other whenever the opportunity presented itself.

The Federal and Confederate Governments were hard pressed to spare enough troops to hold what had been gained in the previous years, and what officers and men were sent to the West were not always the best. One such commander was Colonel J. M. Chivington, an ex-preacher, who led the 2nd Colorado Cavalry in a massacre of a peaceful Cheyenne village at Sand Creek, Colorado, on November 28, 1864. The bloody repercussions of this brutal act were to be felt for over a decade.

Chivington and his troops were hunting roving war parties who had been raiding stage lines, and he was not too particular about the guilt of any Indians he might find. The ex-preacher was a firm believer in the saying "The only good Indian is a dead Indian", and he had publicly stated that when fighting Indians, "Kill and scalp all, big and little, nits make lice." The Colonel's men had captured a half-breed, and Chivington had forced him, under threat of death, to lead them to an Indian village, any village would do. As it happened, the camp they came upon was that of Black Kettle, who had, during the previous August of 1864, been persuaded by the famous trader, William Bent, to keep his people off the war path. But Chivington was Indian hunting and here was his quarry. The 2nd Colorado charged and proceeded to practice what the ex-preacher preached. When it was over, the Cheyenne Chief and some of his people had escaped, but strewn on the ground among the burning tepees lay the bodies of one hundred and sixty of what Chivington called "good Indians". About sixty of this number could be called warriors. The rest were old men, women and children, cut down without mercy, regardless of age or sex.

From that day on, the Cheyenne were bitter foes, attacking the white man at every opportunity. They took the war pipe North, to the Sioux, and the two nations joined as allies. Under the leadership of Roman Nose, a giant of a man, with a nose to match, they derailed trains, raided and burned stage depots, isolated homesteads, and small settlements, such as Julesburg, Colorado, which they left a mass of charred timbers in 1865.

A Look to the West 1862-74

These wild warriors of the plains were natural-born cavalry men, unequalled in the annals of history, with perhaps the exception of the fierce Cossacks of the Steppes of Europe. The massive armies of foot soldiers mobilized during the Civil War were all but useless against the fast moving mounted Indians. What was needed was more cavalry to match the hos-

7th Cavalry Headquarters, Fort Abraham Lincoln, Dakota Territory, 1876.

tiles' mobility on the open plains. In July of 1866, four additional regiments of cavalry were formed, the 7th, 8th, 9th, and 10th. Of the four, the 7th was to leave the most indelible mark on the pages of history. Under the active command of the colorful Lieutenant Colonel George Armstrong Custer, the 7th was quickly forged into a fighting, hard-riding regiment. The men for the most part were rough, largely professional soldiers, ex-officers and enlisted men of both Union and Confederate Armies. What raw recruits there were had been hand picked. They were the type of adventuresome men who, with

3

In the Valley of the Little Big Horn

Hunting and camping party from Ft. A. Lincoln, D.T., at Little Heart River, 1875. Left to right—Lt. James Calhoun, 7th Cav.; Mr. Sweet (son of Leonard Sweet, Chicago); Capt. Stephen Baker, 6th Inf.; Boston Custer; Lt. W. S. Edgerly, 7th Cav.; Miss Watson; Capt. Myles Keogh, 7th Cav.; Mrs. Jas. Calhoun; Mrs. G. A. Custer; Gen. G. A. Custer; Dr. H. O. Paulding, M.C., U.S.A.; Mrs. A. E. Smith; Dr. G. E. Lord, M.C., U.S.A.; Capt. T. B. Weir, 7th Cav.; Lt. W. W. Cooke, 7th Cav.; Lt. R. E. Thompson, 6th Inf.; the Misses Wadsworth of Chicago; Capt. T. W. Custer, 7th Cav.; Lt. A. E. Smith, 7th Cav. (Mr. Sweet and Misses Wadsworth were guests of Gen. and Mrs. Custer).

some rigorous training, could be easily turned into good cavalry soldiers.

Custer drove his men ruthlessly, in on-post training and out in the field. He was the type of commander who could demoralize and ruin a good outfit, except for the fact that he had the knack for implanting in his troopers "Esprit de Corps." When one of Custer's men, wearing the insignia of the 7th Cavalry, hoisted a beer in the local saloon; all who saw him knew he'd been through hell and was ready to go back for more.

The regimental band played a large part in the spirit of the corps, lifting the failing morale of the troops on many a forced

A Look to the West 1862-74

night march and weary day. The band often went into the field with the command and more than once the charge was sounded by the tune of "Garry Owen". *Not to the tune of "The Campbells are Coming"(?)*

Though the 7th saw service up and down the entire frontier, it seemed the destiny of Custer and his troopers was most closely tied to the Sioux and Cheyenne. The 7th is best remembered as a result of action with these two Indian nations. The first of the two major battles was a victory over the Cheyenne, when Custer attacked and destroyed a village on the Washita River in Oklahoma, November 27, 1868. The second engagement was a terrible defeat for the cavalry, one that every school boy has heard of—the battle that ended in tragedy and death for Custer and nearly half of the 7th Regiment. It was fought in the valley of the Little Big Horn against the combined forces of the Sioux and Cheyenne on June 25-26, 1876.

In 1868, after nearly five years of unrestrained bloodshed by both White and Redmen, as a result of the Cheyenne's anger over the massacre at Sand Creek, the U. S. Congress made an attempt to stop the carnage. A military commission was appointed to investigate Chivington's shameful attack on Black Kettle's peaceful camp. The action was eventually publically condemned and the government offered the Indians financial compensation for their losses in the massacre. The white man's coin did not go far however in allowing the spirits of the slaughtered women and children to rest in peace. Too much hatred and death filled the years between the brutal act and the apology. In the Cheyenne's mind, only white man's blood would pay the price, and the hostiles proceeded to collect the debt due at every opportunity.

The year 1868, rather than bring a cessation of hostilities as Congress had hoped, was by far the worst in the four years since Sand Creek. During the summer, there had been twenty-five raids by the Cheyenne, under the hawk-beaked Roman Nose, leaving nearly 125 dead in Kansas, Colorado and Texas. After making a separate peace by treaty with the northern Sioux, the military then commenced to extend a major effort in the south to stop the Cheyenne raids and bring them under control.

Major George A. Forsyth, with a hand-picked battalion of fifty experienced Indian fighters armed with Spencer Carbines, left Fort Wallace, Kansas, to find and engage the Cheyenne on September 10, 1868. On the morning of the 17th, they were chucked from their blankets by the cry "Indians". Roman Nose had been aware of their movements since they left Fort Wallace and had chosen this time and place to attack. Forced to take refuge on a sandy island in the Arikaree River, just over the Kansas line in Colorado, Forsyth and his men fought a desperate battle against an army of Sioux, Cheyenne and Arapahoe, under Roman Nose. They held off charge after charge on the first day. On the second, they faced the great Chief himself, at the head of his hostiles.

As the Indians charged down the river bed in an attack that was sure to overrun them in a matter of minutes, Roman Nose was suddenly toppled from his horse by a fatal shot from the trooper's position. With their leader down, the Indians' charge broke and withdrew. After that, they had no spirit for another frontal attack. Roman Nose had been considered an invincible warrior, with powerful medicine, and had scorned death a hundred times in the last few years. In spite of their great loss, the hostiles had no intention of breaking contact and allowing the slayers of their chief to go free. They held Major Forsyth and his men pinned down on the island for eight and a half days. The troops were finally rescued on the 26th by a column of 10th Cavalry. The beseiged men were near starvation when relief came, and had been forced to resort to eating the putrefying flesh of their dead horses to stay alive during their ordeal. Of the original fifty, there were twenty-three dead or wounded. Among them was second in command, Lieutenant Frederick Beecher, in whose memory the battle was later named "Beecher's Island".

The death of Roman Nose was a great loss to the Cheyenne, as he was the main driving force behind their war with

A Look to the West 1862-74

the whites. But they were to suffer another tragedy in that year, and afterwards, through not completely defeated, they seemed no longer to be effective in their actions against the cavalry.

General George A. Custer and the 7th Regiment U.S. Cavalry had located the area in Oklahoma where the Sioux were wintering. It was the Indians' custom to form a communal winter camp which consisted of a number of small tribal camps spread over a relatively large area. Custer selected one camp on which he would make his attack, and whether by accident

Custer, his wife, and brother Tom

or plan, this turned out to be the village of the unfortunate Black Kettle on the banks of the Washita River. This was the same Chief Black Kettle whose people had been massacred at Sand Creek by Chivington in 1864. The old Chief had now

In the Valley of the Little Big Horn

succeeded Roman Nose as leader of the Cheyenne. Under cover of night on the 26th of November, Custer divided his troops into four battalions, and surrounded the unsuspecting village. At first light, the Oklahoma dawn was shattered by the startling sound of the 7th Regimental Band, as it suddenly blasted out with the tune, "Garry Owen". The troopers poured into the village on four sides, with guns blazing. By ten that morning, all seemed over. Some of the hostiles had escaped, but there were one hundred dead Indians, including Black Kettle and his wife, and once again, many women and children lay among them. Custer ordered the captured village destroyed and had the Indians' horse herd of seven hundred killed. Then, with fifty-three captured squaws and children loaded in wagons, he moved South in an effort to find Major Elliott, who, with nineteen men, had pursued some fleeing hostiles in that direction. (Elliott and his men were never again seen alive. They had been cut off and killed by the Indians from the lower camps who were coming to help Black Kettle.) Large numbers of Indians could be seen massing to the south, gathering from neighboring villages of the communal winter camp, and preparing to counterattack. Before dark, Custer withdrew and picking up his pack train, returned in triumph to Camp Supply.

After the Washita, the Cheyenne were no longer a severe threat in the sounthern plains, though there were some small hot battles fought in the following years which included Cheyenne, Comanche and Kiowa. No powerful leader had arisen after Black Kettle and Roman Nose to unite the hostiles into anything larger than small roving war parties.

By 1874, the Cheyenne and their hostile allies had steadily lost ground till they were forced to the reservation, unable to organize an effective resistance for lack of a leader. Still seething with hatred and anger for Sand Creek and the fresher wound of the Washita, they were like an aimed, loaded cannon—a great destructive force waiting, inert and contained, for the spark that would set them off with a roar, and satisfy

8

A Look to the West 1862-74

their frustrated desire for revenge.

While the Cheyenne were fighting the whites in the southern plains in the years after the Sand Creek massacre of 1864, the Sioux to the north were becoming involved in a war of their own. In 1862, gold had been discovered in Montana. By 1865, there was a desperate need for a supply route for wagons from Fort Laramie, Wyoming, to Virginia City, in the gold fields of Montana. Such a trail was laid out by John M. Bozeman and proved ideally successful, except that it ran through the heart of the Sioux hunting grounds, and the Indians were infuriated by the intrusion. The Sioux, under the leadership of Red Cloud, objected, but to no avail. The usual course of Indian-White relations ensued. Wagons lumbered along the trail—the Indians resisted, blood was spilled, lives were lost on both sides. A blue ribbon of cavalry streamed up the Bozeman Trail, and Red Cloud's war had begun.

The construction of three forts was started along the trail: Fort Reno, Fort Phil Kearny and Fort C. F. Smith. While logs were still being limbed and skidded out of the timber for the palisades, the troopers found themselves fighting for their lives. At the site of Fort Phil Kearny, the timber had to be hauled over open ground from the nearest wood, seven miles away. It was here that Red Cloud made his major effort against his foe. He laid siege to the fort and fought the troops for every stick of wood they hauled. Wood details needed a heavy escort, or they would never return. Not even a wood party of 150 men could feel secure, and casualities were usually heavy. In the first five months at Fort Kearny, 154 men were killed, and over twenty wounded in fifty-one separate hostile attacks. More than half of these casualties were suffered on one single occasion. This was in December 1866, when a young Lieutenant named Fetterman, going to the relief of a wood detail under attack, disregarded his superior's instruction. In a fit of overconfidence, he allowed himself and his men to be drawn into a trap that resulted in the death of his entire command of

Red Cloud's Sioux, with some of their Cheyenne allies, kept a tight ring of death around the fort all that winter, through the spring and into the summer. It was in the summer of 1867 that the famed Wagon Box Fight took place just outside Fort Kearny.

The fort had been dramatically reinforced in the dead of winter, after the Fetterman disaster. Along with additional troops came the Army's first breech-loading rifle, the Springfield Allin Rapid Fire. On August 2, Capt. James Powell, commanding the wood train escort, found himself and almost the entire detail cut off from the shelter of the fort by a large attacking force of hostiles. Powell had his men remove the huge, box-like frames from the wood wagons and arrange them into a rough circle. Then, placing his men inside and covering the tops with tarps so the Indians could not see the number or activities of the defenders, he selected the best shots to shoot, while the others loaded. Fortunately, that morning, each man carried one of the new rapid fire rifles. When Red Cloud led his braves in the first charge on the wagon boxes, they were met by a volley from the defenders. The Sioux weathered the first few seconds of the barrage with heavy losses, but came on, counting on overwhelming the troops before they could reload. With the new rifles, that first volley never ceased, and the hostiles found themselves running into a steady rain of lead. The charge faltered and failed. The Indians were stunned and puzzled. They at first believed they had miscalculated the number of troopers within the boxes. Never having faced troops armed with anything but muzzle loaded rifles before, the Indians had counted on the usual delay to load between volleys to give them time to drive their charge home. Two more charges were met with the same merciless fire, and the Sioux gained nothing by them. Thereafter they contented themselves with moving in and firing on the troops from under cover. When a column from the fort approached with a howitzer, and the full-throated roar of the big gun was added to the steady fire of the rifles, the Indians

A Look to the West 1862-74

withdrew. The relief column was surprised to find so many survivors in Powell's Command. They had lost four wood cutters in the woods during the exchange of fire before the boxes were placed. In the Wagon Box Fight itself, Powell's Command suffered only three killed and three wounded. It was estimated that the Sioux had lost 180 braves in their three attacks.

Despite this serious defeat, Red Cloud and his warriors maintained their stubborn siege on the fort, and eventually gained one of the few true victories of the Indian wars. On April 29, 1868, a treaty commission met with the Sioux and Red Cloud, and agreed to close the Bozeman Trail and abandon the forts. In return, the Sioux gave their word not to interfere with the building of the transcontinental railroad that was to cross the prairie well south of the Sioux hunting grounds. In addition, the Sioux were to have undisputed rights to the Black Hills and Powder River country, forever.

With the southern Cheyenne forced to the reservation, peace finally came to the frontier in the year 1874, after continuous bloodshed for at least a decade. The Sioux were at peace with the Whites by treaty. The Cheyenne, Comanche and Kiowa had been forced to their knees and held in check. The gates westward were finally opened.

CHAPTER 2

The Long Trail

WHEN THE NINE YEARS after the Civil War can be looked on in retrospect, it is plain to see how victory over the hostile Indians was accomplished. With the border states and territories in complete chaos after the war, the military plunged in, and spent three years fumbling and feeling the situation out. 1868 is the year it seemed apparent that a simple effective plan was decided upon. It was one that could not fail if it could be put into action. It was "Divide and conquer."

In 1868, the two most powerful hostile nations were the Sioux and Cheyenne. The Cheyenne stained the southern plains red under the bloody Roman Nose, while the Sioux fought in the north led by Red Cloud. Both hostile nations aided each other. Then the government carefully and successfully took the Sioux out of the picture by the concession made to Red Cloud in the treaty of 1868. The Sioux leaders were able to tell their people they were victorious. Hostilities ceased, as the white man withdrew from his forts, and closed the Bozeman Trail, leaving the Sioux the opportunity to live in much their old normal manner on their native soil. Though they still had warriors in the South with the Cheyenne, it was but a token force of war parties, having little effect. Next, an attempt was made to placate the Cheyenne with the condemnation of the five-year-old Sand Creek massacre, and financial retribution for the Indians' losses was paid. But the Cheyenne were not satisfied and the military exerted a major effort to force their capitulation. Whether by design or accident, their two main leaders, Roman Nose and Black Kettle, had been

Custer's column, 7th Cavalry, forming up during the Black Hills expedition 1874. Note the large number of supply wagons, as well as beef on the hoof needed to support a full scale expedition.

In that country, - the edge of the Black Hills - one could march, -(ride) - all day, and never see a tree. E.W.O.

eliminated, and during the next five or six years, the Cheyenne were slowly forced to submit.

Then the "Great White Fathers" in Washington, with the pressing necessities of an active Indian war off their hands, desired a second look at what had been so freely offered to the Sioux in return for peace in 1868—the Black Hills of Dakota.

Brevet Major General Custer and the 7th Regiment, the same that had destroyed the camp of Black Kettle on the Washita, were sent to explore and map the area in the summer of 1874. They had several brushes with the Indians dur-

The Long Trail

ing the expedition, for the Sioux were angered by the presence of cavalry in their sacred hills. This was minor though, compared to the news that Custer brought back. It was not long after the regiment's return that the newspapers across the nation carried the screaming headlines heralding the news of Gold in the Black Hills. The spark that the Cheyenne had long awaited had been struck. Whites poured into the Sioux land. The treaty of 1868 was trampled under the miners' boots. Again the usual course of White-Indian relations followed— intrusion, bloodshed, death, cavalry. The Sioux must now pay for the six short years of peace they had enjoyed. The white man was ready to take back what he had said was to be theirs forever. The Cheyenne on reservations to the South knew what would now follow, and left the agencies in large numbers to aid their Sioux brothers, and in doing so to finally gain their full measure of revenge for Sand Creek and the Washita. Fate had one last gift for the Sioux and Cheyenne before the bitter pill of final defeat must be swallowed. They were granted one more chance to meet Custer, and the 7th, on the field of battle.

By late fall of 1875, the government had become greatly concerned about the increasing number of Indians leaving their reservations. Reports had it that they were gathering under the leadership of two of the Sioux's greatest men, Sitting Bull of the Hunkpapa, a talented organizer and tribal leader, and Crazy Horse of the Ogalalas, a peerless warrior recognized not only by his own people the Sioux, but by the Cheyenne as well.

In November of that year, General Alfred Terry, commanding officer, Department of Dakota, U. S. Army, sent an ultimatum to Sitting Bull. He demanded that he bring his people back to the reservation by January 1, 1876, or he would . . . "come looking for him." The reply from the great Sioux Chief was as short and clear as it was ominous. "You won't need to bring guides. You can find me easily. I won't run away."

By March of 1876, there was no indication that the Indians

15

In the Valley of the Little Big Horn

had any intention of complying with General Terry's order. So on March 17th, though the countryside was still locked in the icy grip of winter, General Crook left Fort Fetterman with ten troops of cavalry and two companies of infantry to find the hostiles, and test their strength and determination to follow their haughty chief.

That year in Montana, the month of March was bitter cold, and no time to expect man or beast to be on the move without the requirement of absolute necessity. Above all, to the Indian mind, it was no time to wage war. From the time the oldest of the old ones could remember, and even before, winter was for the warmth of the tepee or lodge, the fire and the deep pile of the buffalo robes. It was time for the making of tools and weapons and much talk; a time to eat, rest and gather strength for the wildly active summer life of the Plains Indian.

Crook found an Indian trail near the Powder River and sent Colonel Joseph J. Reynolds with six troops of cavalry to follow it. When Reynolds found an Indian village near the mouth of the Little Powder River, he prepared to attack at once. His first charge caught the Indians off guard and by complete surprise. With the unbelievable din of a cavalry charge ringing in their ears, they burst from the tepees, many of them naked from sleeping robes, only to have their eyes attest to the incredible truth their ears had told them. In the bitter cold of that March day, the troopers drove the unprepared Indians from the village. With the hostiles' horse herd in possession, the soldiers began to burn the tepees and lodges to complete their victory, leaving those Indians who had escaped with nothing but their lives, and the hastily grabbed weapons held in rapidly numbing fingers.

But this was the village of Crazy Horse, who had gained a splendid reputation for bravery and courage at the siege of Fort Phil Kearny during Red Cloud's war. He rallied his defeated braves with fierce counter charges and led them back into the burning village. The troopers, surprised and stunned, retreated in such haste that they left their dead and wounded behind,

The Long Trail

along with the Indians' horses. The angry Sioux pursued the fleeing column and eventually succeeded in capturing the command's herd of beef cattle.

General Crook was forced to return to Fetterman for supplies, but he had the answer he had been sent to find. It would take a full scale campaign to defeat and move the stubborn Sioux, and it would be a long hard-fought one. Other than that, no good had been accomplished. Reynolds had succeeded only in burning a few tepees and killing some Indians, along with a number of his own men. But worst of all, the anger of the hostiles and their fearsome war chief had been raised to white hot heat; that must be quenched in blood before there would be peace in the northern territories.

With the final passing of winter and the advent of spring, an expedition designed to once and for all break the back of Sioux resistance to white authority got under way. The plan was to execute a giant pincer movement with three separate commands. Colonel John Gibbon was to leave from Fort Ellis, Montana, with part of the 7th infantry, Gatling guns and some of the Second Cavalry, a total of approximately 400 men. General Altred Terry was to move west from Fort Abraham Lincoln, Dakota territory, with Custer and the 7th cavalry, nearly 600 strong. General George A. Crook, with a force of more than 1,000 men, was to move north from Fort Fetterman, Wyoming. The three armies were to converge on the hostiles somewhere in the southeast corner of the Montana territory, and gain their surrender, or crush them.

General Crook started north once more as planned. He picked up and followed, in general, the trail that Colonel Reynolds had taken some three months earlier. Crook expected he would have to meet and deal with Crazy Horse again, somewhere along the way. His suspicions were soon confirmed when he received a message from the Chief, warning him that if he dared cross the Tongue River in Montana with his soldiers, he would be attacked. The column moved steadily on, until, upon reaching the appointed river, the command made

17

In the Valley of the Little Big Horn

camp without crossing. General Crook stayed encamped for four days, awaiting the arrival of three hundred Shoshone Indian scouts. Finally, with their number swelling his original force, Crook took up Crazy Horse's challenge, and crossed the river. The troops marched without incident to the Rosebud River. On June 17th, after a night's encampment on the river bank, they started down stream with their scouts out. About midmorning, they had reached a wide place in the valley sur-

Remington Cap and Ball, Mod. #1858 Army, found at the site of the Rosebud fight. This was a common side arm of the Indians in 1876. It was, no doubt, lost by a Sioux warrior during the battle.

rounded by bluffs. The effect was that of coming into a natural arena. The Rosebud plunged down a shadowy gorge to the right and disappeared from sight. It was here that Crazy Horse chose to do battle.

The sound of gun shots ahead of the column brought all heads up. In a moment, the scouts came back from over the bluff at breakneck gallop, yelling "Sioux, Sioux, heap Sioux." As officers tried to halt their panicky flight, the skyline around them seemed to sprout Indians, until every bluff and ridge in sight was feathered with Sioux warriors. The crack of rifle fire began to grow continuously. The troops swung into a battle line to return the hostiles' fire by volleys. The Indians held a superior position, being on the bluff tops and able to fire down on the troops from all sides. Crook ordered a charge to dislodge

The Long Trail

them. Captain Anson Mills and Captain W. B. Royall led their companies up the steep bluff sides under a rain of arrows and bullets. The Sioux were forced back. The charge was halted at the bluff top as the Indians regrouped a short distance off, and both sides welcomed reinforcements. Then suddenly, as was typical of Crazy Horse, who seemed to need a stinging blow struck against him to make his already simmering fighting blood come to a boil, the Indians charged. Less than half of the warriors had firearms, and desired close quarters to do the most damage, using tomahawks, knifes and lances. The Sioux came on at full gallop, crashing into the massed troopers and the two armies melted into one mass of stabbing, clubbing, jabbing, shooting men, on plunging horses. From its midst rose a great swirling cloud of dust and smoke. The air was split with the bark of guns, the screams of horses, yells of troopers, and the hair raising war cry of the Indians. The battle poured over the edge of the bluff and rolled down the slope like a living avalanche of mounted men.

As the struggle spread on the bottom land and the Sioux seemed to have gained the upper hand, a well-timed charge by Captain Guy Henry and his company averted disaster. In doing so, however, Captain Henry was shot from the saddle, and only through the extraordinary bravery of Chief Washakie and some of his Shoshone scouts was he saved from capture and certain death at the hands of the hostiles.

When the pace of the fight momentarily slackened, Crazy Horse took the opportunity to disengage and withdraw from the field, going down the ravine where the Rosebud cut through the bluffs. Crook was tempted to follow after them, in the hopes of finding the Sioux village at the other end, and destroying it. Before he had gone far, however, he reconsidered and withdrew, fearing that the wily chief could well have set a trap for him in the canyon's gloomy depths. His premonition was right, for Crazy Horse had laid an ambush there, that would have truly earned the foreboding name the place already bore, "Dead Canyon of the Rosebud".

General Crook's force had been sorely hurt. One day of fierce battle had shown him that the hostiles before him, with Crazy Horse for a leader, were more than he could handle with his present command. Though Crook had won the field that day, Crazy Horse was the true victor, for he had stopped Crook in his tracks. The next morning, June 18th, Crook began the long withdrawal back toward his base of supply at Goose Creek, Wyoming. The southern jaw of the Pincer had been dulled and broken.

Crazy Horse was satisfied that Crook had been soundly defeated and was no longer a threat. He now felt free to move his people over the divide, between the Rosebud and the Little Big Horn to join the already huge encampment of Sitting Bull.

For the first time in the history of the Sioux nation, all its major tribes had gathered in one place, setting their tepees and lodges side by side as allies in a common cause. There were Ogalalas, Hunkpapas, San Arcs, Minneconjous, Santees and Brulës. They welcomed their brothers the Cheyenne and even some Arapahoe. They were all welded into one mighty force by Sitting Bull, and would be led into battle by Crazy Horse, Gall, and other great war chiefs of equal ferocity but lesser reputations. They all had but one goal in mind, to break the strangling grip of the white man's hated authority over their lives.

Sitting Bull had meant what he said when he had sent word to General Terry that "You can find me easily. I won't run away." The trail to the great camp in the valley of the Little Big Horn was wide, clear, and dusty, with the recent passing of many feet. The determined chief could not have beckoned Terry to come any more clearly if he had sent him an engraved invitation along with a marked map and compass. There could be no mistake about it, the Sioux, all of the Sioux and a great many Cheyenne, meant to fight, not run.

While the southern arm of the Pincer under General Crook was engaged in combat with Crazy Horse, General Terry was on the move westward. Major Marcus A. Reno, second in command of the 7th Cavalry under General Custer, had been sent on ahead with six troops of cavalry as an advance probe, and discovered a large Indian trail in the vicinity of the Rosebud River. The Major returned immediately to the main column and reported his find to General Terry. On June 22nd, the entire command reached the Rosebud River, where it empties its waters into the Yellowstone. Terry did not know that the carefully planned pincer movement had already been ruined. General Crook had met the Sioux on the 17th, had been defeated, and was by this time five days on the trail back toward Goose Creek, carrying his wounded.

General Terry and the 7th had followed, first the Missouri, then the Yellowstone Rivers, from Fort Abraham Lincoln. They had been paced all the way by the river steamer, *Far West*, which had acted as a supply ship. Upon arriving at the mouth of the Rosebud, they were joined by Colonel Gibbon, his infantry, cavalry and Gatling guns from Fort Ellis.

On the evening of the 22nd, a meeting was held in the cabin of the steamer. Present were General Terry, Colonel Gibbon and Major General Custer. During the meeting it was decided, having had no word from General Crook, that they would follow this plan—General Custer would take the 7th Regiment and move up the Rosebud. When he came upon the trail Major Reno had discovered, he was to determine if it led over the divide into the valley of the Little Big Horn. If so, he was to send word back immediately, via the scout named Herendeen, and then move up the river one day's march (*The Rosebud*). before crossing into the Little Big Horn valley with his men. In the meantime, General Terry would accompany Colonel Gibbon's slower moving column, consisting mostly of infantry, down the Yellowstone to the mouth of the Big Horn, then up ~~down~~ the Big Horn to the Little Big Horn. It was expected he would arrive there on the 26th or 27th of June. The plan was to catch the Indians in the valley between the two commands and if possible, persuade them verbally to return to their reservations peacefully. Only if they refused to cooperate would

In the Valley of the Little Big Horn

force be applied. It was at this time that General Terry attempted to impress on Custer that he should time his march so as *not* to arrive in the valley before the 26th, as he and Gibbon would not be in position to carry out the plan before that time. Terry even suggested that Custer take the Gatling guns with him. Custer refused the offer saying that they would only slow him down, and that he believed he, with his 7th Regiment, could handle any situation that might arise.

General Custer had recently incurred the displeasure of President Ulysses S. Grant, as a result of some of his political activities in the east. Grant had ordered that Custer should not even accompany the 7th Cavalry in the coming campaign, let alone command it. Upon the plea of Custer that he be spared the disgrace of being left at the fort while his regiment went into action, General Terry interceded on Custer's behalf. President Grant finally relented and advised Terry that if he thought Custer was indispensable, he would allow him to go. Thus, when the 7th left Fort Abraham Lincoln, Custer was at its head. Terry knew the impetuous nature of Custer and his weakness for committing his troops to rash acts. He therefore did everything in his power, short of direct blunt orders, to insure Custer's compliance with the agreed plan.

When the word spread that the 7th was to separate, Mr. Mark Kellogg, special correspondent for the *Bismarck Tribune,* sought and received permission to accompany them. In anticipation of the adventure to come, he sent this dispatch to his paper: "We leave the Rosebud tomorrow and by the time this reaches you, we will have met and fought the Red Devils, with what results remains to be seen. I go with Custer and will be at the death." No one knew at the time, how prophetic these last words from Mark Kellogg were. Three days later, he was among the dead on the Custer Battlefield.

General Custer prepared his command to move ahead. He ordered that each man carry, in addition to the usual 24 rounds of pistol cartridges, 50 rounds of 45-70 rifle ammunition on his person and 50 rounds in his saddlebag. He had instructions

The Long Trail

passed to the trumpeters that they were to sound no bugle calls until further notice. The clear Montana air would carry the piercing note of a bugle for many miles in all directions, distinctly announcing the presence of troops many hours in advance of their arrival.

On the morning of the 23rd, <u>Captain Benteen</u>, who had pack train duty that day, looked to the final preparation of the animals, as the head of the column led off across the river. All the gear necessary to the sustenance of a cavalry regiment in the field; food, ammunition, oats, medical supplies, spades, axes, leather and tools for the saddlers, pots, pans and kettles for the cooks, hammers, tongs, forge and anvil for the blacksmiths, horse shoes, nails, files and other tools for the farriers and a hundred additional items, were packed and snugged on the backs of 160 mules by the five citizen packers, with the aid of the pack train detail. The pack detail, which was made up by drawing six men from each of the twelve companies of the regiment, watched their buddies ride on in a column of twos. They must lag behind, cursing their luck, and nursing the stubborn, frustrating mules along every foot of the way.

Sometime after the column nosed its way across the Rosebud River and turned upstream, they struck the trail of Crazy Horse and his people. The Indians had passed there a few days earlier, on their way over the divide to the valley of the Little Big Horn. The dust lay two and a half inches thick on the beaten track, indicating that many feet, both horse and human, had passed.

<u>General Terry's instructions to Custer</u> were for him to <u>send back word</u> by Herendeen, advising Terry of the direction and expected destination of the trail. Though Herendeen came to ride at Custer's side and waited expectantly, the General rode on <u>in silence</u>. He was apparently determined to follow the trail to its end, confident of another <u>smashing victory</u> for "<u>Custer and the 7th</u>". He hoped <u>a victory</u> would <u>return him</u> to the <u>good graces of President Grant</u>, or at least rekindle the <u>flame of admiration in the hearts of the American people</u>. On the trail,

In the Valley of the Little Big Horn

they found an Indian campground that had been deserted but four days earlier, and here they counted the marks of four hundred cook fires. The General was elated with his find. He had come looking for hostiles, and from all the fresh signs, there would be plenty to go around. Custer had supreme confidence in his regiment and their ability to handle any number of Indians with ease.

In his column rode <u>his brother, Captain Tom Custer</u> of C Company, and his brother-in-law, Lieutenant James Calhoun with L Company. These two men were professional soldiers and danger was part of their everyday lives. Custer could not have suffered the slightest apprehension of disaster, as attested to by the fact that he allowed yet <u>another brother, Boston Custer,</u> and his nephew <u>Arthur Reed</u> to accompany the troops. These two young men were civilians and had come along, not because it was their duty, but rather for the pleasure and excitement of the trip.

General Custer drove his men hard, spurred on by addition of many smaller trails to the main track. It was much like many tributaries in feeding a great river like the Missouri, creating a flow of immense proportions and widening its path as it traveled on.

The troops had come two or three hundred miles in the last thirty days, and men and horses were sorely worn. Heedless of their condition because of his zeal to get at the Indians, General Custer ordered long, hard wearing forced marches. It was said of the General, that he could ride all day at a killing pace, sit up half the night or more, talking or writing letters, and then leap into the saddle, fresh and rested in the morning, to lead his command on another grueling ride that would leave his men and officers staggering with fatigue. He seemed to have a hidden well of energy when obsessed by a specific aim, and could push on endlessly in this manner, without rest, stopping only briefly and impatiently, when his men could go no further.

The command had been in the saddle most of the day of the

24

The Long Trail

24th and then broke camp again at 11 P.M. that night. After two and a half hours on the trail approaching the divide, his scouts managed to convince him he could not cross over in the

Custer seated with guide and Arikara scouts during the Yellowstone Survey. The Indian on Custer's right is Bloody Knife.

dark. Frustrated, this time by the forces of nature, Custer reluctantly ordered a halt, but would not allow the horses to be unsaddled, for as the trail grew hotter, so did he, and cared not to waste the time it takes to saddle a horse. The General summoned Mr. F. F. Girard, interpreter, and the two scouts, Half Yellow Face and Bloody Knife. By this time, the troops were pouring scalding coffee from bubbling pots and munching hardtack to appease their growling bellies, or stretching their bone

25

In the Valley of the Little Big Horn

weary frames on the unyielding earth to sleep and soothe their bleary eyes and brains. But Custer, impatient to push on, though physically with them, was already mentally over the divide and probing for clues as to what tomorrow, June 25, 1876, would bring to him. He asked interpreter Girard's opinion as to how many Indians they might encounter. Girard replied that he expected the hostiles numbers would not exceed 1500 to 2000. *They were probably nearer 8,000.* EMO

With the first light of dawn, General Custer left his camp with Mr. Girard and the two scouts to climb the divide and survey the valley for himself. On finally gaining the heights, *I know Varnum* they met Lieutenant Varnum, commander of the Indian scouts *later,* who called their attention to smoke in the distance. Through *EMO* their binoculars, they could pick out some teepees and Indian ponies, but could make no realistic estimate of the size of the camp or number of Indians that might be present. The scouts had reported it to be a very large village, and also that they had encountered hostile scouts on the divide.

While the General was in the mountains, a sergeant asked for, and received permission to return along the column's back trail in an attempt to locate some misplaced belongings. He was not gone long, however, when he burst back into camp at a gallop, and reported to Captain Yates that he had seen some hostile Sioux on their back trail. In Custer's absence, this report was passed on to the regiment's Adjutant Cooke.

General Custer came off the mountain and met his command, already moving along the trail, at about 10 A.M. He halted them and sent word to his officers by orderlies, that he desired an "Officers Call". This command was commonly announced by the appropriate bugle call, but in compliance with the General's orders of three days previous, it was passed instead by word of mouth. When the officers had assembled, he briefed them on their situation, telling them that the scouts had reported sign of a large village in the valley of the Little Big Horn; but that he thought they were mistaken. He said that he had been to the mountain top and had looked through his

The Long Trail

glasses and "saw nothing." The command moved on; the Little Big Horn River was now less than twenty miles away. The hoofs of the horses and mules thudded on the battered earth as they strained to carry their weight and that of their burden of man or pack, up and over the barrier of the divide. Then both man and beast leaned back against the pull of gravity, swaying from side to side to the steady jog of the iron shoes on the path, as they slowly descended, stiff-legged, into the valley.

Moving along on fairly level ground again, a huge dust cloud rose from beneath their feet and hung above the column like a gigantic plume, a great deal of it coming from the shuffling mules. General Custer sent Colonel Cooke with instructions for Captain Mathey to move his pack train off the trail and proceed alongside. The trail was now smothered with a four to five inch coat of dust, that rose in billowing swirls, like smoke, with each step. But just off to either side, the ground was firm and though a little rougher going, the animals could pass without filling the air with powdered earth.

About twelve noon, after penetrating the valley by about a mile and a half, Captain McDougall was ordered to move B Company to the rear of the column and take command of the pack train. His duty was to help keep the train moving along and to act as rear guard.

Captain Benteen was then instructed by General Custer to send an officer and six men ahead and to the left as far as a line of bluffs, about four or five miles away. The Captain was to follow them at a rapid pace with D, H, and K Companies and was to "Pitch into anything they found, and send back word immediately." At about 12:10 P.M., Captain Benteen left the main column at a 45° angle, heading south-west. Major Reno saw Captain Benteen's column separating and asked him where they were going. The Captain replied that he had been ordered by General Custer to move to the distant bluffs, driving everything before him.

Major Marcus A. Reno, being second in command of the

27

In the Valley of the Little Big Horn

regiment, had duties that carried him up and down the long column, lending support, advice and counsel to other officers and men wherever needed. He normally had no company to command, but was bound to aid General Custer in the operation of the entire regiment, whenever and however it was required. So, when the Major received the General's orders to take personal command of a battalion consisting of A, G, and M Companies, and to proceed along next to the General's column, he did so, without question or hesitation.

This completed the division of the regiment into four separate commands. Captain McDougall was far to the rear with B Company and the pack train. Captain Benteen with D, H, and K Companies had disappeared in the rugged terrain to the left. Major Reno rode at the head of his column, containing A, G, and M Companies and General Custer and his Field Staff, including Adjutant Cooke, Assistant Surgeon, G. E. Lord, headed up the remainder of the regiment.

At this time, none of the battalion commanders, including Major Reno, had been advised of any over-all plan or maneuver Custer might be contemplating. Each had been given instructions separately, and no one knew what the other's function was to be.

The two columns, headed by Custer and Reno, rode on for eight or nine miles, separated by a shallow, narrow ravine that cradled a small creek on its way to join the Little Big Horn River. Mr. Girard, the interpreter, who was flanking Custer's column by a few hundred yards, upon mounting a high bluff, found an old tepee with a dead warrior inside. There were other signs that indicated that this was an Indian camp site very recently evacuated. When he lifted his eyes from the task of reading the sign on the ground surrounding him, he was rewarded with a view of the valley of the Little Big Horn. There was the river, the open grassy plain cut by small ravines and gullies. To his right and left on his side of the water ran a jumble of erratic bluffs and ridges, while in the distance a light haze softened the rude edges of distant hills.

The Long Trail

The bottom of the valley was spotted with irregular patches of cottonwood timber and something else that made him leap up, standing straight in his stirrups. Snatching his hat from his head and waving it wildly, he "hallooed" to Custer, yelling, "Here are your Indians, running like devils". This is what Custer had expected. It was, he believed, necessary for him to act swiftly now, before the Indians had time to elude him completely. General Custer immediately ordered the scouts to advance towards the village ahead of the troops. The scouts did not share Custer's contempt for the force of Sioux they were about to meet, and refused to go on almost to a man. They had a better opportunity than most to take a good close look at Sitting Bull's village. They judged the hostile numbers to be considerably larger than Custer did, though they could not convince him of that. They also did not believe the hostiles were running away, but rather felt sure they were waiting for the troops and preparing a warm reception. In short, they judged the regiment's chances of survival, if they charged the village, to be exceedingly poor, and they wanted no part of the action.

General Custer, angered by what he considered to be the cowardice of the scouts, ordered them to dismount and surrender their arms and horses. He then signaled Major Reno to bring his column across the ravine to join him.

The Major, in complying, led his troopers down into the cut. The distance was not far, nor was the ravine deep; but the going was so rough that when he led up the opposite bank he was at the tail end of Custer's column. Colonel Cooke was waiting for him there and told him the General wanted him up front. He and his battalion moved forward. As Reno drew to the front of the column, he saw only about 25 or 30 of the Indian scouts, dismounted and applying war paint, in preparation for battle. Apparently Custer's ultimatum to obey orders and move forward, or surrender their weapons and horses, had some limited results.

At this time, General Custer had no idea of the actual size of the encampment, or number of warriors they were to encounter, but Custer with his customary contempt for the enemy, especially the Indian, must have believed that the sight of his beloved 7th Cavalry in a stone-shattering charge would panic the devil himself at the very gates of hell. Thus, he prepared to make his rash move with but 600 men. The hostile force was later estimated by scout George Herendeen at 3,500, while the Indians claimed 9,000 warriors. All were contained in an encampment that stretched to a length of close to three miles and was from a few hundred yards to a half mile wide. In addition, it was Lieutenant Wallace's opinion that the Indians had been aware of the cavalry's approach from the time it crossed the Rosebud River, some three days before. The element of surprise, a great asset in any attack, was nonexistent. Besides the fact that the 7th Regiment was scouted by the hostiles from the time it crossed the Rosebud, the command approached the encampment over high ground and along the bluffs. If the Indians did not see the troops themselves, they could not have missed the ever-present dust cloud.

When Major Reno reached the front of the column, he received his orders from General Custer. The exact wording and manner in which the orders were delivered vary slightly according to witnesses. Mr. Girard recalled having heard General Custer say to Major Reno, "You will take your battalion and try to bring them to battle and I will support you," and as Reno was leaving, the General allegedly shouted after him, "And take the scouts with you." Lieutenant George D. Wallace, acting regimental engineer, testified that he had heard Adjutant Cooke give Major Reno the General's orders this way, "The Indians are about two miles and a half ahead on the jump. Follow them as fast as you can and charge them whenever you find them, and we will support you." Girard testified he had also heard the orders given to Reno by Cooke, in essentially the same wording as Wallace had, and added that he heard the Major say "Is General Custer coming along?" Cooke's reply was "He will support you." Major Reno himself, when testifying before the Court of Inquiry, stated that he did

The Long Trail

not remember speaking directly with General Custer, but was given the General's orders by Adjutant Cooke. To the best of the Major's recollection, the Adjutant said, "General Custer directs you to take as rapid a gait as you think prudent, and charge the village afterwards, and you will be supported by the whole outfit."

Though the exact wording of the orders that Major Reno received from General Custer cannot be determined, there is no room left for doubt that General Custer believed that at this time the hostile Indians were fleeing from him, and that he had ordered Major Reno to pursue and attack them, assuring him that the prompt physical, military support would be forthcoming—where, when and if it was needed. Major Reno, with the understanding that this was to be a direct frontal attack on a retreating foe by the major portion of the regiment, led his battalion at a fast trot for two miles to the waters of the Little Big Horn River—and into the pages of history.

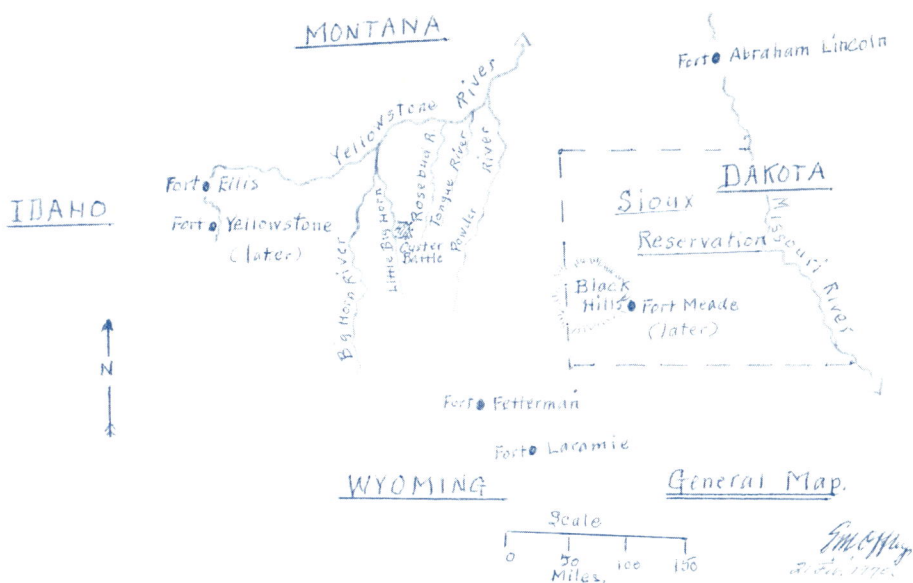

31

Custer took his five troops four miles down the east side of the Little Big Horn River, — far beyond supporting distance of Reno.

It may be only fair to Custer to say that his attack, though late and far distant, did draw off many of the Indians who were about to annihilate Reno's command and made it possible for the latter to get back across the river and up on the bluff where joined by Benteen, McDougall and the pack train, he held out until Terry and Gibbon arrived on the 27th of ~~July~~ June.

Edward M. Offley.

CHAPTER 3

Major Reno's Charge

CAPTAIN BENTEEN and three companies were out of sight and touch, some miles to the left. B Company and the pack train were under the command of Captain McDougall falling further to the rear. Major Reno with three of the eight remaining companies acted on his orders and moved ahead to make the attack. He believed he would be followed and supported by Custer and the balance of the regiment. Upon separating, Reno's battalion was joined by what few scouts had the courage to follow their commander, Lieutenant Charles Varnum, and his aide, Lieutenant L. R. Hare. This included interpreters, scouts and guides, such as F. F. Girard, George Herendeen, Half-breed Billy Jackson, the famous white scout Charles Reynolds, and interpreter Isaiah Dorman. The latter two were killed later that afternoon in the valley. Dorman was a Negro who had lived among the Sioux for a number of years and was married to a Sioux woman. He was in the employ of the government at Fort Rice, and was with the expedition as an interpreter. Among the few Indian scouts who did not desert the troops were Stab, Bobtail Bull, and Bloody Knife. All three never left the valley of the Little Big Horn, where their bones still lie.

As the command approached the ford in the river, Mr.

Girard, riding in his usual position a little forward and to one side of the column, encountered one of the Indian scouts, who seemed in great haste to leave the valley. Girard stopped and questioned the man, and was told by him that the hostiles were moving up the valley in force to meet the troops. As the first horses of the column splashed into the waters of the Little Big Horn, Girard reined in beside Reno on the river bank. Major Reno and Mr. Girard were not on good personal terms at the time, as a result of a dispute between the two men that had taken place back at Fort Abraham Lincoln. Thus, when Girard volunteered the scout's information, all he got for his pains was a cool glance from the Major. Reno stated later, during the Court of Inquiry, that it was not Mr. Girard's place to give him scouting reports, as he was an interpreter only, and that he had no confidence in the truth of anything Girard might say. Girard, irked by Reno's unappreciative attitude, wheeled his horse about, and set off at a gallop along the back trail to give his unsolicited information to General Custer. He had not gone far, however, when he met Adjutant Cooke riding toward him alone. Cooke asked where he was headed. Girard told of the Indians' movements, and Cooke instructed him to return and report to Major Reno, while he (Cooke) would advise General Custer of these new developments. They turned about and separated, each riding in the direction from which they had come. What evaluation was made of this information and what effect it may have had on Custer's plans is hard to ascertain. Major Reno, however, had his orders; he was to pursue the Indians and give battle, and he proceeded to carry them out.

The water at the ford was horse belly deep, and the formation of the battalion was thoroughly disrupted in crossing. The horses were allowed to drink sparingly and the troops were called to reform upon reaching the far bank. Major Reno placed A and M Company on a battle line with G Company in reserve. At the command, the battalion moved forward at a fast trot that soon became a gallop. Men and horses were still exhausted from the past three days of forced marches, and only

Major Reno's Charge

the excitement of the rapidly approaching battle kept man in the saddle, and horse pounding turf. As the two-mile gap between Indian and Cavalry rapidly closed, Major Reno could see, that rather than fleeing, as Custer had told him, the hostiles were preparing to meet him in what he judged to be superior numbers. He instructed his striker (body servant), Private Archibald McIthargey from I Company, to deliver his compliments to General Custer, whom he thought was immediately to the rear, and inform him that "the Indians were in front of him in strong force."

The ground shuddered under the charging horses and heart beats took up the rhythm of the drumming hoofs. The first scattered shots from the hostiles cracked above the rumble of the charge. Distance shrank, time flew, and still no word from Custer. Major Reno then dispatched Private John Mitchell, a cook detached from I Company, with the same message, "Indians in front in strong force." He directed his Adjutant Lieutenant Hodgson to bring the reserve, Company G, up on the battle line. With Major Reno and his officers out in front, they came on again at a dead gallop. The battalion was spread out in a solid line of grim-faced, determined troopers, on a hundred and twelve snorting horses.

The Indians were raising a big dust at the edge of the village. It was still impossible to estimate their number or even the size of the camp. The dust swirled and flowed in eddies, as mounted Indians appeared from its opaque heart, circled and whirled, fired at the troops, and then were swallowed by the boiling cloud. Tepees would materialize in its depths, as the dust thinned in spots, only to melt away again as a fresh broil rolled over them.

Major Reno had been in Indian country a long time and his experience told him that these odd tactics by the hostiles could mean but one thing, "TRAP"! He could see that an effective charge could not be executed and that he would accomplish nothing but casualties for his men. The only alternative he had was to assume a defensive position.

The dust cloud trap was undoubtedly to miss lead Reno into believing they were pulling out but Reno knew his Indians too well to be deceived. EMO

In the Valley of the Little Big Horn

Reno gave the command to halt, and it was echoed up and down the line by his officers. Troopers hauled back on the reins. With arched necks, flaring nostrils and rumps down, the horses set their powerful legs, filling the air with turf, stones and dust. Iron-shod hoofs ripped the sod skin of the plain, as the pounding rhythm of the charge came to a shuddering halt. The commands to dismount and skirmish were punctuated by the increasing hostile fire. G Company made the right of the line, A Company center, M Company the left. The skirmish line stretched from 75 to 100 yards across the plain with the right anchored on a crescent-shaped patch of cottonwood timber. Every fourth man was designated "horse holder" whose job it now was to lead, tug, or coax the excited mounts into the protection of the timber. For the first time that day, the heavy thunder of the cavalry's 45-70 Springfields began to answer the lighter bark of the Indians' Winchesters.

The scouts had fired the first shots returning those of the enemy as the skirmish line formed. But as the number of hostiles before the troops began to grow to an uncountable mass, nearly all the remaining Indian scouts unashamedly fled the field to a safer position. They had stayed only long enough for the Sioux to confirm what they already knew and could convince no one else of; that this day belonged to the free, wild Sioux warrior of the old times, not the white invader and his turncoat Indian scouts.

The land itself seemed to disgorge warriors from her very bowels. From each canyon, gully and dry creek bed they came, finally rebelling against the brutal rape of mother earth by the white man, who plundered her mineral wealth, sheared her crowning glory of primeval forests, and scarred her lovely face with the iron-tipped plowshare. One might think that she could stand no more of the presumptuous white creature, who thought he might claim a part of her as his own personal property, by driving stakes or laying fence, and now was sending her children in countless numbers to drive him off. The Indian lived in unison with nature and did little to change the

Major Reno's Charge

way of things; rather, he adjusted his life to conditions. When he moved on from one area to another hunting or camping ground, he left little evidence that he had been there that would not disappear in a short while. The place returned to mother nature and was unspoiled and available to the next man who cared to set his camp kettle there. But not so with the white man. When he chose a spot to settle in, he stripped the land of trees, plowed the earth, built a wooden house and fences, telling the world that this land was his forever, and its use was free to no man, without his permission. Thus, the Indians poured from their hiding places to fight for this great, wild, free land that had been theirs from the dawn of time, and was now being taken inch by inch, never to be free to them again.

The hostiles came at the troops from behind the foot hills, out of the almost invisible, dust-enveloped village, and up from a ravine that was ten yards wide, four or five feet deep, and lay about three or four hundred yards ahead of the skirmish line. The trap that Major Reno had sensed was obvious now to even the rawest of recruits. The dust makers had been the tempting bait, in an ageless Indian tactic. Pretending to be confused and completely disorganized, they offered the troopers easy victory so as to draw them on into the grasp of their hidden comrades. Five or six hundred Sioux had been waiting in the ravine for Major Reno and his 112 men. Later at the Inquiry, Reno commented that "If we had continued to charge, most of the saddles would have been emptied and most of the horses killed." Lieutenant DeRudio of A Company put it in even stronger terms when he said, "I saw that we would have been butchered if we had gone 500 yards further." A good cavalry horse with an experienced rider may have been able to leap the ravine, but a good many of the horses and troopers were green, and there had not been much time to train and season them. Even if some had successfully cleared the ravine, they would have jumped into the waiting arms of the dust makers. The ones unfortunate enough to stumble into the chasm would have instantly gone down, man and horse, under a mass of swinging clubs, knives and hatchets, like men engulfed in quicksand. Those few who might have managed to remain in the saddle, after finally stopping their charging mounts and wheeling to flee, would have been easily overtaken by the hordes of Indians on fresh ponies and pulled down, one by one, in short order.

It was now between 2:30 and 3:00 o'clock in the afternoon. The troops had come from an expected victorious charge, to a skirmish line, in desperate defense of their lives. The experienced old timers fired with deliberate slow care, trying to make each shot count, while the new men, letting the feverish heat of combat possess them, fired as fast as their fumbling fingers could load. The 1873 Springfield would shoot long and straight in the hands of a competent soldier, but eight or nine rapid shots by a frantic rookie would often result in the failure of the ejector. This being the case, some men found themselves picking with sheath knives at a shell jammed in the chamber while hostile bullets sheared their buttons and spat sand in their faces.

The officers worked hard to steady the men and control their fire. A slow advance was started and the far end of the line stepped out. But the men of G Company on the right, next to the timber, were reluctant to put much distance between themselves and the sheltering wooden arms of the trees. The result was that instead of a straight advance, the skirmish line pivotted on the timber, the far end moving about 75-100 yards. The hostiles would ride within range to empty their lever action rifles into the troopers' ranks and then fall back to reload their weapons. They were thick in front and moving to the left to begin a flanking fire. Anxious eyes flicked to the rear at every opportunity, searching in vain for General Custer and his promised support. Then the light-colored flanks of the gray horses of the Gray Horse Company, a part of Custer's battalion, caught the mid-afternoon sunlight and flashed it through the swirling pall of dust and smoke into the searching eyes of Lieutenant Varnum. The action in front of the line was fierce and growing more so. The Indians were not only to the left but slipping to the rear as well. There was time for only a fleeting glance, but there could be no mistaking what Varnum saw; it was Custer's column all right—but not at all where he was expected. Instead of arriving on the scene with aid, the General was on the high bluff on the far side of the river two miles away, moving down stream, away from the desperate plight of Reno's Battalion.

The only other man to catch sight of Custer's Command from the skirmish line was Private Edward Davren of F Company, who claimed he had seen General Custer, Colonel Cooke, and one other man on the highest bluff across the river, a short while later. The three men waved their hats as though cheering, and then went down out of sight. Though the distance was considerable, Davren said he could identify them because of their garb. Both General Custer and Colonel Cooke had on blue shirts and buckskin pants. All the other officers and men of the regiment were wearing regulation jackets and trousers. When Davren saw Custer waving his hat, he assumed the General had seen them, was cheering them on, and would join them shortly which, of course, he never did.

With the Indians moving around the left end of the line, and to the rear, Major Reno took G Company with him into the woods to prevent the possible loss of their mounts. Upon exploring the timber to evaluate its defensive qualities, it took the Major but a few minutes to determine that their position was precarious. In the timber's center there was a fair size clearing surrounded by a fringe of trees, some of considerable size. Reno determined it would be necessary to hold the outer edge of the woods in order to keep the Indians on the open plain; otherwise, they would have crept up under the cover of the trees and been right on top of them. Because of the extent of the timbered area, it was Major Reno's opinion that it would take six or seven hundred men to do the job. Perhaps the whole regiment could have made that position defensible, but only for as long as the ammunition lasted. The Major summed it up with these words during the Inquiry, "I saw I could not stay there, unless I stayed forever."

With the constant arrival of additional hostiles, and the rapid diminishing of ammunition on hand, the situation on the skirmish line was growing critical. In the ten minutes of hot action that had taken place, some of the men had fired nearly all of the fifty rounds they carried, and troopers were being sent back to the horses to bring up the fifty rounds each man carried in his saddle bags. The skirmish line had been outflanked; with the enemy on the left, in front, and to the rear, the line was withdrawn into the shelter of the timber. The opinion of Sergeant F. A. Culbertson of A Company was this, "If the skirmish line did not withdraw when it did, in three minutes, no one would come off it alive."

Upon reaching the comparative safety of the timber, Lieutenant Varnum met a half-breed scout and asked if he could take a message back to General Custer. The scout replied in sign language, moving his hands in front, on the sides, and in back of him, indicating that they were surrounded and no one could get out.

The troopers were holding the Indians at bay on the plain, but suffered under a heavy fire from the enemy, as they dashed back and forth on their horses. Up stream, where the timber stretched a brushy arm along the river bank, the Sioux were entering and working their way in force toward the battalion; while from the other side of the river, the hostiles threw a rain of lead at the soldiers among the trees. Smoke began to billow from the underbrush where the Indians had set fires in the hope that the flames would flush their foe out into the open.

Major Reno now found himself living a commanding officer's nightmare. His battalion was completely surrounded by an enemy force that outnumbered his men by ten to one. His ammunition, food and water were not sufficient for a long siege, plus the fact that he had only one-sixth the men neces-

Major Reno's Charge

sary to successfully defend the position he held. The promised support was long overdue and apparently not coming at all. He had been advised of no plans that General Custer may have had, but had simply been ordered to attack with three companies what he had been led to believe was a fleeing foe. He had also been assured of support by the whole outfit. Reno had made the ordered attack, and was forced to assume a defensive position, alone and unsupported. Nothing could be gained by remaining where he was, other than the eventual senseless annihilation of his entire command. He made the only decision that sanity would allow, "We have to get out of here—we have to charge them!" The question was, where might they take refuge? After a brief consultation with his officers, he chose a bluff that rose about 100 feet above the waters of the Little Big Horn on the far bank. There they would stand a better chance of making a successful stand and might attract the attention of the rest of the regiment.

Major Reno instructed his Adjutant, Lieutenant Hodgson, to pass the word to his company commanders, Captains Moylan, French, and Lieutenant McIntosh, that the battalion would charge through the encircling Indians to the high bluff across the river as soon as the men could be mounted. "Men to your horses. The Indians are in our rear!" was the cry that brought troopers to their feet and on the run for their mounts. The companies formed in a column of fours as best they could in the clearing within the timber. Major Reno was talking to Bloody Knife, concerning the hostiles' movements, when the faithful Indian scout was struck and killed by a shot from among the trees close at hand. He had been standing so near to Reno at the time that the latter was spattered with the scout's blood when he was hit. The timber nearby began to pop like a kettle of corn as the Indians closed in under cover. With the cry of, "My God! I've got it," a trooper jerked upright, then slid from his saddle. Reno instinctively barked the order, "Dismount". This was the standard method for cavalry to combat a foe on foot and close at hand. But the Sioux were

When there was not time to execute the command; - "Fight on foot," - see note on page 36.
E.M.O.

In the Valley of the Little Big Horn

coming through the timber in force and being more cunning in woodcraft than the cavalry trooper . . . "would have made short bloody work of them." Before all the boots in the stir-

This is the point on the Little Big Horn where, after the timber fight, Reno and his battalion crossed in their retreat to Reno's Bluff on the right. The white marker in the foreground is where Lieut. Hodgson fell. The marker on the horizon is where Dr. DeWolf died.

rups could come to the ground, Reno gave the counter command, "Mount", and led the column out of the clearing and through the woods to the edge of the plain. He held them there for nearly ten minutes, waiting for stragglers, until the fire from the hostiles became so severe that they could wait no longer.

With Major Reno at the head of the column of fours, the

Major Reno's Charge

battalion charged out into the open ground and down the barrels of the Sioux guns. Most of the troopers slipped their single shot Springfields into saddle scabbards, and drew their Colt Revolvers for the close fighting ahead. The ranks had formed with A Company first, then M Company, trailed by G Company. The front of the column was in good order, but part of M Company and all of G Company, lacking room in the timber while under fire to form up properly, got off to a ragged start and were poorly organized. As the head of the column struck out at the hostiles between the timber and the river, the massed Indians unexpectedly parted, avoiding physical contact for the moment. But the Sioux now stood in large numbers on both sides of the column, creating a corridor through which the battalion must pass. Major Reno and his men found themselves running a bloody "gauntlet." Standing off between 50 and 100 yards with their Winchesters across their horse's necks in front of them, the Sioux fired into the column as fast as they could crank the levers, not caring much whether they hit horse or man, for a dismounted man on that Indian-filled plain was as good as dead. Even above the thunder of hoofs, the belching of guns, and the wild yipping of the Indians, troopers could hear the sickening whack of slugs as they struck the bodies of comrades or tumbled horses end over end in a cloud of dust.

Captain Moylan of A Company saw the mount of one of his troopers collapse under him, sending the man headlong over its neck, to tumble like a broken doll on the hard earth. Then with a titanic effort, the trooper forced his bruised body up, to regain stumbling, but reliable feet. With the determination that only the fierce will for survival could provide, the stunned trooper caught the flying reins of a galloping, riderless horse from G Company, and swung into the blood-stained saddle. On the run, he slipped between the fingers and out of the grasp of the clutching hand of death. There were many more who were not so fortunate that day.

The Sioux contented themselves with raking the well-formed

head of the column with fire from a distance. But as the disorganized scattered rear came up, they closed in to point-blank pistol range, fighting hand to hand. Troopers and Indians alike were dismounted, as thumb-size fingers of lead punched through yielding flesh and shattered bone. Men of White and Red skin, locked in each others' vice-like grips in their furious struggle to the death, lost their mounts and came crashing to the ground between the dancing legs of panic-stricken horses. Wounded and dead lay where they fell, for to stop a second to aid a wounded or struggling comrade would mean certain death to the "Good Samaritan!"

As Private Davren of F Company broke from the timber after the main part of the column left, he urged his mount to its utmost speed in a frantic attempt to catch up with the battalion. Before him lay a scene of complete chaos and horror. The ground in the wake of the rapidly receding column was strewn with the bodies of horses and men, some in the blue uniform of the cavalry troopers; others almost naked, copper toned skin glinting in the sun, heads crested with colorful feathers. Over all hung a ground mist of beige dust and blue-grey gun smoke. The rumble of thousands of horses' hoofs pounding the earth was like the beat of kettle drums laying a background for the staccato rattle of gunfire and the high pitched piping yells of the Indians, accompanied by the intermittent screams of horses and men. It all melted into one ear-splitting sound, like an over-long crescendo at the end of a horror-filled symphony. Mounted Indians darted in all directions, shooting and clubbing at the scattered troopers who made up the trailing end of the column. Two men from G Company who had lost their mounts were trying to run the "gauntlet" on foot, and were being closed in on by several mounted Sioux. Davren swung his mount in their direction to give what help he might in passing. As he came close, his horse stumbled, throwing him over its head, to slam down on the scarred turf like a sack of meal. As he raised himself from the ground, he saw that the Indians had jumped the two troopers

Major Reno's Charge

and dragged them down. There was nothing he could do for them. He caught the bridle of his stunned horse as it got to its feet, and managed to mount and ride clear, catching the shattered rear of the column as it bunched up at the river's edge.

The bank of the river at the point where the battalion found itself attempting to cross was five or six feet high, and the horses had to be forced with spurs and curses down into the water. The Sioux once again stood off a couple of hundred yards and fired their rifles as fast as they could work them into the milling mass of troopers.

Lieutenant Hodgson jumped his mount off the bank into the water, but was unhorsed in doing so. He found himself in waist-deep water with thirty or forty yards of river to cross, while bullets kicked up small geysers all around him. He had started to push his way across when a mounted trooper offered him a stirrup and hauled him over and up the steep bank on the opposite side. As he started on foot for the hilltop, he was cut down and killed by a bullet fired from a high bluff nearby. Dr. DeWolf, the acting Assistant Surgeon, who had successfully completed the hellish ride and crossing, was also killed by shots fired from the top of the same bluff when he started up its side, mistakenly thinking it was the one they were to take refuge on.

The last of the troops cleared the river, while the head of the column caught its breath at the top of the one-hundred-foot rise. The climb had been steep and difficult, and the hill side had been salted with shot from the hostiles on the far bank of the river. Many of the horses were so exhausted that they could not carry their riders up the slope and had to be led and coaxed to the summit.

The Sioux did not follow the battalion across. Unexpectedly they began to move off down stream without apparent reason. If the hostiles had persisted in the attack, it was the opinion of many who were there that they would have gotten them all, to the last man. *They had probably received word in some way that Custer was about to attack their camp some miles down stream. EMO*

In the Valley of the Little Big Horn

For the first time in three quarters of an hour the men of Reno's Command were not living under a hail of deadly lead. With the arrival of the last troopers to come up on the bluff,

Mr. John S. duMont pictured sitting at the head of the water carrier ravine which runs from Reno's Bluff to the river (1953).

the afternoon air ceased to be ripped by gunfire. They had lived through forty-five minutes of pure hell! Though the foe and the sound of battle were gone, the trail of the "gauntlet" was clearly marked across the face of the plain, from the timber to the bluff top, with the dead bodies of troopers, Indians, and horses. Seven wounded men had somehow kept to their sad-

Major Reno's Charge

dles and completed the murderous ride. Over twenty-five per cent of the battalion were killed, wounded or missing, in the three-quarter-mile charge out of the timber to the bluff. There was at least one trooper killed and two wounded in the timber, plus the chief guide and scout, Charley Reynolds; Interpreter, Isaiah Dorman, and the Indian scout, Bloody Knife. The roll call on the bluff top after running the "gauntlet" showed these results: A Company, 8 killed, 5 wounded; M Company, 8 killed, 2 wounded, and G Company, 11 killed. It is not clear whether some of these men listed as killed at this roll call were among the troopers left in the timber. Thirteen soldiers, three of whom were wounded, two civilian interpreters and a half-breed scout all managed to find their way back to the command within the next two days.

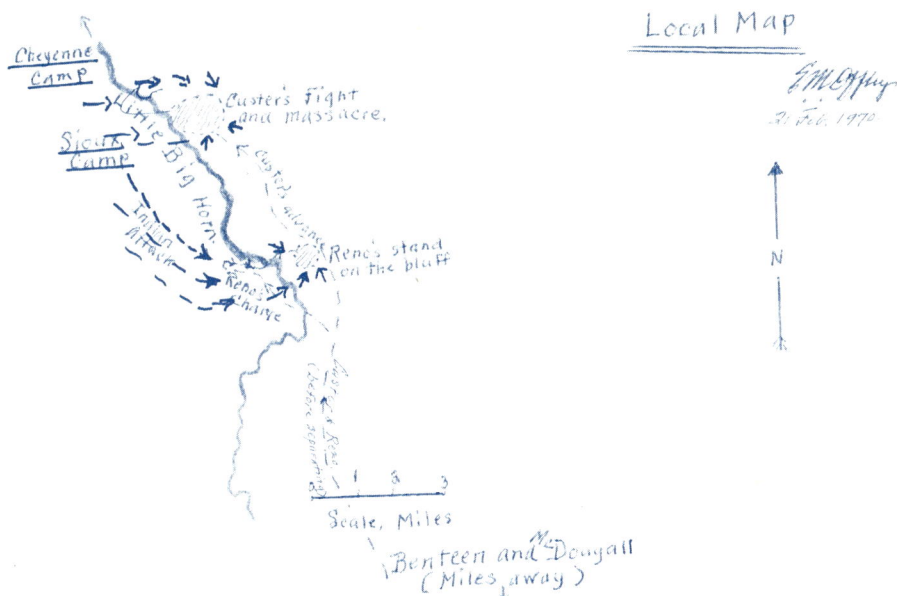

Why did Custer break up the normal organization of his regiment, i.e., three Squadrons of four troops each; 1st Squadron; Troops A.B.C.D. 2d Squadron; Troops E.F.G.H. 3d Squadron; Troops I.K.L.M.; — each Squadron under a Major or Senior Captain? Each one of Reno's three troops came from a different squadron. Was it to keep the troops in which his relatives were serving with him, — (Custer), — possibly for the reason I have surmised on Page 64, — see also Page 24? How I wish Godfrey, Hare and others I knew were still living and might be able to answer my question!, including Custer, himself,

Edward M. Coffley
November, 1970.

CHAPTER 4

The Reunion

MAJOR RENO and what was left of his battalion took refuge on the high bluff overlooking the valley of the Little Big Horn. About ten minutes after the last of his battered troopers arrived, Reno was relieved to see Captain Benteen and his command of approximately 120 men making their way up the southeast side of the hill to join him. The Major spurred his horse to meet them, and noticed on the way a fresh trail left by shod hoofs that could only have been made by Custer's Column. The trail ran just behind the bluff Reno had taken position on and headed downstream, or roughly due north.

When the two commanders met, the first question each had for the other was concerning the whereabouts of General Custer and his men. Major Reno showed Captain Benteen the trail that had just been found. He told him he had been sent to charge the Indians on the plain. Custer's instructions to the Major through Adjutant Cooke <u>implied that he (Custer) would support him with the whole outfit</u>, and that was the last he had seen or heard of him. Reno still had no idea where Custer was.

Captain Benteen's information was little more satisfying as all he could offer was that he had been sent by Custer to find

In the Valley of the Little Big Horn

a valley off to the left that was not there and instructed to drive everything before him. He also showed Major Reno <u>a dispatch</u> he had <u>received from Custer</u> a short while before, which read, "Benteen, <u>come on</u>, <u>big village</u>, <u>be quick</u>, <u>bring packs</u>. P.S. <u>bring packs</u>" signed "<u>W. W. Cooke</u>". Up to this point, neither officer had known what the others orders were, and no one knew what plan Custer had, if any, or where he had gone.

There was a good deal of speculation, grumbling and cursing among the enlisted men, now that they had time to think about something other than staying alive. Many felt that Custer had put them in a disastrous position and then run off leaving them to their fate. Most of the officers felt that the General had made an attack of his own, had been driven off and had withdrawn downstream toward the mouth of the river. It was assumed that he was attempting to join forces with General Terry's columns which would be coming from that direction.

Major Reno's intention, in view of the overwhelming number of hostiles he had encountered, was to reunite the regiment as soon as possible. But first, there were wounded that needed the attention of Dr. Porter; and the pack train which could be seen approaching must be brought up. It carried not only the food and medical supplies, but most vital of all, the supply of ammunition on which their lives would depend.

The first of Custer's fateful orders was to Captain McDougall. He was instructed to take B Company to the rear and assume command of the pack train. Then about 12:10 P.M., Captain Benteen was instructed through Adjutant Cooke, with the General's compliments, to <u>take command of companies D, H, and K;</u> and with an officer and six men in advance proceed rapidly to a line of bluffs to the left, and four or five miles in front. He was to pitch into anything they found and send back word immediately. Captain Benteen separated with his battalion, leading them to the left as ordered, at about a forty-five-degree angle; while Custer, Reno and the eight remaining

50

The Reunion

companies of the regiment followed the Indian trail on toward the river.

We will now follow the action of Captain Benteen's battalion, which took place while Major Reno and his command

Capt. F. W. Benteen

were fighting their desperate battle in the timber and across the plain. After moving at a trot for about a mile, Captain Benteen was overtaken by a courier in the person of the regiment's Chief Trumpeter, Henry Voss. He had additional instructions for him. Voss told the Captain that it was the General's wish if they found nothing by the time they reached the first line of bluffs, they were to go on to the next. The terrain they were in was very rough, making it necessary for them to pass through many defiles and detour around ravines and bluffs. On completing their second mile, they still had found no trace of Indians. Once more they were overtaken by a trooper on a lathered horse. This time, it was Sergeant Major William Shorrow, with still more instructions from Custer. It

In the Valley of the Little Big Horn

was <u>the General's order</u> that upon reaching the bluffs he had been directed to, Benteen was to <u>proceed into the valley,</u> and if he found nothing <u>there</u>, was to go on to the next.

The battalion pushed doggedly on, over three more difficult miles. Upon reaching the appointed bluff, the advance party reported back from the top that they could see no sign of a valley or Indians, only more broken, rugged country. By this time, Captain Benteen was convinced that Custer could not have had any knowledge of the lay of the land. If he had known the terrain, he never would have sent him here, looking for Sioux. In Benteen's own words, "Indians had more sense than to go any place over such country." Thinking that he might be needed back with the regiment, as the trail they were following when he was detached was large and fresh, he made the decision to turn his column to the right and attempt to intercept the regiment's line of march.

At just about this time, the regiment had come in sight of the village, and under the orders of General Custer, Reno with three troops was fording the Little Big Horn to start his charge on the hostiles. Despite the fact that Custer, during his officer's call in the morning, stated that he did not believe the reports of the scouts concerning the presence of a large Indian village in the valley of the Little Big Horn, Benteen stated that, "He had an idea that General Custer was mistaken about there being no Indians in the vicinity."

The Captain led his battalion at a stiff pace, anxious to make contact now that he had made the decision to rejoin the regiment. After some few miles, they stopped to water the horses at a boggy morass, and as the column was leaving, the first mules of Captain McDougall's pack train jogged into view. The thirst-crazed mules, smelling water, rushed into the morass before they could be stopped, and several were hopelessly mired up to their packs. Benteen could see that it would take some time to haul them out, and feeling confident that no Indians could get to the pack train without first running into him, pushed on. By now, unknown to Benteen, Reno's Bat-

The Reunion

talion had made contact with the Indians and was on the skirmish line, fighting for its life.

Benteen soon picked up the regiment's trail and moved on quickly. The Captain had a very fast walking horse and when it stepped out, as the Captain let him do now, the column had to stay at a trot to keep up. They moved on smoothly for about seven miles, until they came upon the bluff where stood the lone tepee of the dead warrior. This was the point where Girard, about one hour earlier, first sighted the village and reported to Custer that the Indians, . . . "were running like devils." The tepee had been set ablaze by Arikara scouts who had not crossed the river with Reno. The horses had passed another mile under their noses when Sergeant Kanipe of C Company, Custer's Battalion, reined in before Captain Benteen. He reported that he had been sent by General Custer to hurry the pack train along. The Captain figured that the pack should be clearing the morass just about now, and told the Sergeant that the train was under the command of Captain McDougall, and that he would find them about seven miles along the back trail.

Sergeant Kanipe saluted Captain Benteen and spurred his horse to a fast trot, down along the column to deliver his message. As he went, he shouted to some of the men, "We've got 'em." Wisps of dirty, gray smoke could be seen in the air over the valley beyond the bluffs. This was from the fire set in the underbrush of the timber by the hostiles in hopes of driving Reno into the open during the battle. But with the Sergeant's encouraging words, it was easy to visualize a burning Indian village as its source. Captain Godfrey, for one, was sure by all indications that Custer had attacked and defeated the Sioux, and was burning the village. He was so sure, in fact, that when he finally arrived on Reno's bluff, which he assumed was a picket post to protect the troops at work in the village, he was shocked when Lieutenant Hare, in reply to Godfrey's query said, "They had a big fight in the bottom and got whipped like hell!"

[Handwritten marginal notes:]

Benteen must have been separated from Custer some 10 or 12 miles, with the 3 ammunition teams, etc., much more distant. EWO

(who was with Benteen)

Later on, Godfrey, (Edward S.) was my Lieut. Colonel, (12th Cavalry) and Hare, (Luther R.), was a Major, Commanding the Squadron in which I, as a Lieutenant, Commanded F troop. EWOffley.

In the Valley of the Little Big Horn

The pack train had, in general, followed the trail toward the ford taken by Custer and Reno; and Sergeant Kanipe found them a few miles behind Captain Benteen's column. The Sergeant bypassed Captain Mathey at the head of the train and rode to the rear, where Captain McDougall and B Company

Capt. Mathey

were riding rear guard. Kanipe delivered his message to Captain McDougall, who immediately employed his troop to aid in closing up and pushing the lagging mules to a trot. By now, Captain Mathey could see the smoke in the valley also and had no idea what it meant, except that Custer must have made contact with the hostiles. When he saw a half-breed scout hurrying in the opposite direction to where the river lay, he took the opportunity to find out what was going on. He asked the scout if "General Custer were whipping them?" The reply was, "They were too wary for him." On this ominous note, Mathey sent word to the rear, suggesting that Captain McDougall have his troopers help close up the train. Mc-

The Reunion

Dougall by this time had received the message from Custer via Sergeant Kanipe and in ten or fifteen minutes was at the head of the column at Mathey's side, with the train closed up and moving in good order behind him.

Two miles from Reno's ford, Captain Benteen halted his column to receive a courier, Trumpeter John Martin. As the dust settled back to the ground about the horses' hoofs, Martin saluted and delivering General Custer's compliments, handed Captain Benteen a written dispatch. After reading "Benteen, come on, big village, be quick, bring packs. W. W. Cooke." "P.S. bring packs", he folded the paper and tucked it in his jacket pocket. The Captain asked Martin about the village and the whereabouts of Custer. Martin replied that the Indians were "skedaddling", and he didn't think there would be much need for the packs, and that by now he supposed Custer had made a charge through the village. Though Trumpeter Martin on his ride from Custer to Benteen could see Reno's battle with the Indians from the high bluff, he did not volunteer this information, as Captain Benteen did not ask about Reno's Battalion. The fact is Captain Benteen, at this time, did not even know that Major Reno had a command of his own, and that Reno and Custer had separated. After being dismissed by the Captain, however, Martin was overheard by an officer telling Captain Benteen's orderly that General Custer had found a large village and, ". . . Major Reno was attacking it, killing men, women and children."

Captain Benteen set off at a fast pace along the Reno trail toward the ford and the rising column of smoke. When he arrived at the ford well in advance of his battalion, he received a most unpleasant shock. Across the river on the plain writhed the cavalry blue and the red men in deadly combat. He sat his horse like a bronze statue, for a moment a stunned witness to the bloodiest part of Major Reno's charging retreat. He believed what he saw was the whole regiment in action and that they were being "Thrashed!" He estimated that there were 900 Indians on the plain and with horrified eyes saw them hitting the shattered end of Reno's column and "Charge through them again and again." His eyes traced the bloody trail across the bottom land to the chaotic mass of troopers backed up and attempting to ford the river. The Captain's attention was then caught by a small knot of Indian scouts a short distance away on his side of the river. Among them was "Half Yellow Face," who was gesturing wildly, drawing his attention to a high bluff nearby. There at its top he could see the head of Reno's column beginning to gather. As his battalion came up, he turned them right about, and along the back trail, to lead them up the southeast side of Reno's bluff.

Immediately upon the union of Captain Benteen's battalion with Major Reno's command, they exchanged intelligence as to the dramatic events just enacted, and the mystery concerning the whereabouts of General Custer. Major Reno then dispatched Lieutenant Hare with instructions to the pack train. Its dust was in sight, moving at a fair pace in their direction. The Lieutenant careened down the steep trail, knowing that he carried a message that could well mean life or death for the men he left behind. Though Benteen's battalion had not, as yet, seen action, and each man still carried 100 rounds for his rifle, plus 24 for his pistol, the troopers of Reno's command had less than half of their ammunition left. They had used up *over* 6,000 rounds in about three quarters of an hour of very hot fighting. Should the hostiles return in force and pin them down on the bluff for any length of time before they were re-supplied, they would find themselves fighting with rifle butts and skinning knives before they were struck down in death.

Lieutenant Hare had whipped his horse to its limit of endurance by the time his sagging mount drew up in front of Captain McDougall and Mathey. He told them briefly what had happened and delivered Major Reno's urgent request for ammunition as fast as possible. Two mules were immediately out of the line, each carrying two boxes of ammunition with one thousand rounds per box, and driven at a gallop to the

The Reunion

bluff. The rest of the pack train followed as fast as good order would permit.

The two battalions now stood united on the hill top, under the command of the senior officer, Major Marcus A. Reno. The ammunition mules were in the perimeter and troopers were replacing the spent cartridges while the balance of the pack train came on. With its arrival, Major Reno would have more than half of the regiment, and all its supplies, under his command. For the moment, all of the Indians had left the plain and ridges that could be seen from the bluff. The only shooting that could be heard was faint and distant, down river. Not all of the men heard it, but there is no doubt that there *was* action in that direction, and that it was Custer being engaged. Private Davren claimed that he saw some of the action on the Custer battlefield, four miles away. Of course, at this distance no details could be distinguished, but he may have seen the movement of mounted men on the plain. From the testimony, and his identification of Custer and Cooke at a distance of approximately two miles while in the timber, Davren must have had eyes more like an Indian than white man. Lieutenant Edgerly was one of the officers to hear the distant gunfire, and he discussed it with Captain Weir of D Company. They agreed that it must be General Custer, and from the sound of the firing, he did not seem to be in desperate straits. They thought that his attack might be repulsed, as Reno's was, but it did not enter anyone's mind that his command would be cut up and wiped out to the last man. Captain Weir, knowing the desirability, if not the necessity, of joining up with Custer and his five companies, told Edgerly that he was going to find Major Reno and ask permission to take D Company and attempt to effect a liaison with General Custer, but Weir could not find Reno, for when the Major heard that his Adjutant and good friend, Lieutenant Hodgson, had been hit while at the river, he had taken a few men down to find him in hopes that the Lieutenant was only wounded and might yet be saved. He found Hodgson's body where it had fallen, and seeing that he was beyond help, collected the Lieutenant's personal effects for his next of kin, and started sadly back up the hill to carry out his responsibilities to those still living. Captain Weir, not being able to find Major Reno, returned to his company, called his orderly, mounted his horse, and as Captain Benteen put it during the Inquiry, "Captain Weir sallied out in a fit of bravado, I think, without orders." When Lieutenant Edgerly saw his Captain mounted and leading off along Custer's trail, he assumed that Weir had secured permission for them to go. He called the troopers of D Company to horse and followed after him. Weir kept to high ground along the spine of the bluffs, while Lieutenant Edgerly held the troop to a lower level where the going was easier for a large body of mounted men. They proceeded in this manner for the distance of about one mile to the highest bluff along the river. Shortly after arriving, Weir was joined by Captain Benteen and Godfrey, who had followed with their troops almost on the heels of D Company. From their high perch, the officers could see the slightly rolling, broken, bad lands of the Custer battlefield. The area was infested with Indians riding in all directions and occasionally shooting at unidentifiable objects lying inert on the ground. There was a ragged ravine here that cut the bluff and ran like an ugly scar down its face in the direction of the Little Big Horn River. Weir led his troop into it, and started down, accompanied by the clack and scrape of the horses' iron shoes on the rock-strewn floor.

When Major Reno came back on the bluff after finding Lieutenant Hodgson's body, he instructed Lieutenant Varnum to take a detail down the hill and bury him. On their way down, they met Mr. Herendeen, a civilian interpreter and scout, with 11 troopers, all walking. These 12 men, three of whom were wounded, had been left in the timber during the retreat, either because they had lost their mounts or had not heard the order for the charge. At least four more men were still alive back there: Lieutenant DeRudio, Sergeant O'Neill, Interpreter Girard, and half-breed scout Billy Jackson. The

The Reunion

latter two still had their horses but DeRudio and O'Neil were on foot.

Before Lieutenant Varnum and his detail could carry out Reno's orders to bury the body of Lieutenant Hodgson, he was recalled to the top of the hill. It had now been about one hour since the first of Major Reno's battered battalion reached the bluff, and now the last of the pack mules were coming in. With plenty of ammunition on hand, and the pack train safely back in the protection of the fold, Reno made the final preparation to follow after Captain Weir to find, and join, General Custer if possible. Captain Moylan and A Company were detailed to carry the wounded at the rear of the column. The method employed to transport them was the best that could be provided at the time. Having no litters, or even materials available to make travois, they had to carry the men in blankets. By placing one man at each corner and two at the center, they hauled the suffering men along with as much gentleness as this tedious, clumsy manner would allow. No matter what torture this caused the wounded men, it was far better than being left behind to the "tender" mercies of the vengeful Indians. As a result of their exhausting burden, Captain Moylan soon found his detail falling too far behind for his comfort. He asked for, and received, more help.

As the slowly moving column approached the high bluff from which Captains Weir and Benteen viewed the Custer battlefield, heavy firing could be heard in the ravine that had swallowed Captain Weir and D Company. Shortly, Captain Weir came back and reported to Major Reno that he had seen no sign of General Custer, but had been met by an overwhelming force of hostiles and had taken the liberty of using the Major's name to order a general withdrawal. Reno concurred with the Captain's decision and decided the best action to take was to return to their original position on the bluff top they had just quit. The column was turned about in its tracks and started on its slow way back.

As Captain Weir's troop erupted from the mouth of the

ravine and spilled back over the crest of the high point, a guidon was firmly planted there to serve as a rallying marker for Custer's command in the valley below. No one suspected

Custer's Last Stand area looking toward Weir's Point (arrow) in the distance.

that the eyes for which this marker was placed had been already forever closed.

As D Company moved back along the trail in a fighting retreat, Lieutenant Edgerly came upon a helpless wounded trooper. There was no time to spare to give aid, as the hostiles were forcing them at a steady rapid pace. The Lieutenant told the trooper to crawl into a nearby hole for cover and promised he would come right back to save him. Edgerly found Captain Weir, told him of his promise to save the wounded man, and asked for permission to throw out a skirmish line so he

The Reunion

could bring him in. Captain Weir now found himself in the unenviable position that is the painful burden an officer must bear: to comply unquestioningly with his orders, regardless of personal feelings. He replied that he could not allow it. When Lieutenant Edgerly insisted that he had promised the helpless man he would be back, Captain Weir replied, "I cannot help it! The orders were positive, to go back on the hill, and we must go back!" The wounded man was engulfed by the hostiles like a pebble on the beach in the face of a rising tide, waiting desperately for the promised aid which never came.

As the troops of the combined command filed back onto the bluff top, Major Reno placed them in a defense perimeter. He knew that shortly they would be subject to a fierce assault. He called Captain McDougall and B Company from their duties with the pack train and ordered the pack detail on the line with their respective companies. Crates of ammunition were brought, opened and placed near the line in positions where they would be easily available when needed. When the Major directed Captain McDougall to place B Company, he told him to "Hold at all hazards." During the fierce fighting that followed, McDougall said of his men, "I saw no man show the 'White Feather' or any indication of fear at all." As each man flattened himself and squirmed down in an attempt to gain as much cover as possible on the barren hilltop, Captain Godfrey and K Company came in, just ahead of a hail of bullets. Captain Godfrey had taken it on himself to dismount his company and form a skirmish line that fought a gallant rear guard action, allowing the rest of the command to take position without heavy casualties. In holding the eager hostiles at bay, he doubtless saved many lives.

It was near six o'clock in the evening now, and the surviving troops of the 7th Regiment, roughly 340 men, were as ready as possible, and waiting to face thousands of Sioux warriors. Though it was the best available, their position left a lot to be desired. The battalion lay on a 100 foot bluff in a shallow depression. Cover was scarce. The mules and horses were placed in the center of the dish-shaped hilltop, but even this was not adequate shelter. When the Indians could find no part of a trooper to shoot at, they pelted away at the animals, killing many. Room was made for the wounded men in the center of the herd, and they were barricaded with boxes and crates of supplies.

For three hours the scant defenses of the battalion were pelted and peppered by a "galeing" fire that Lieutenant Wallace described as a "continuous roar." If a trooper showed any part of himself, he immediately became a target for heavy fire. Casualties began to mount as the late afternoon wore on. Captain Benteen's company, located on a slight knoll, was hardest hit. Before the day ended, he had 20 men wounded and two killed. The lever action Winchester made up the bulk of the Indians' arms and fired several rapid shots to the Springfields' one. The Indians not only had many times the fire power but over three times as many men, and they did not appear to suffer from a lack of ammunition. It seemed as if they were determined to blow the top off the bluff with rifle fire, and they kept at it until darkness shrouded their sights and hid their targets. As luck would have it for the luckless 7th, June 25, 1876, was the longest day of the year in that latitude, and darkness did not come until after 9 P.M.

The sun set as a huge red ball in the West and as the echoes of the last shots died away, a heavy black cloak of darkness spread its folds over the bluff and valley. The violent sights and sounds of that horror-filled day were smothered in the night, only to be replaced by a more ghastly vision. The sun seemed to be reborn again in the valley, first as a tiny spark, then a bright flame that swiftly grew into a dancing red giant as the hostiles kindled a great bonfire in view of the beleaguered troops. The night air carried to the troops the first soft beat of the drums that grew louder and louder, until the very ground they lay on seemed to take up the throbbing rhythm. Dark figures leaped and gyrated, silhouetted against the roaring flames and the night was split with the screams and howls

The Reunion

of the scalp dance. Did not the lances sprout multi-tip tines? Could not a man see the cloven hoof on the prancing, goat-legged dancers, while the tips of their head horns shot sparks of light into the air and their spear-pointed tails snapped like whips? Who could say these were not all the fiends of hell, soaking their black souls in an orgy of blood and fire, as they prepared a place for each trooper in the white hot embers of that hellish flame.

With this picture burned forever in each mind, and spurred on by the bone-chilling cries that sliced up the bluff side to their ears from the valley of death, the troopers fell to the task of scraping rifle pits in the hard ground with tin cups, knives, hachets, and bare hands. On Major Reno's orders, saddles, crates, boxes, and even dead horses and mules were dragged to the line to be laid as breastworks against what the drums told them would come with the dawn.

Major Reno considered the possibility of attempting to move off the hill during the night but decided against it. He was sure there would be fighting, and though they no doubt could break loose with a charge, this would require the abandonment of the wounded. They had well over 30 wounded troopers who could be moved only with slow and deliberate care. To leave them behind would be unthinkable. Reno felt he could hold this position now that they had weathered the merciless fire of the previous evening and had time during the night to build some defenses. He knew that Generals Terry and Custer had planned to meet at the mouth of the Little Big Horn River on the 26th or 27th and that relief should be coming up river soon. Among the command were some few remaining Indian scouts and Reno attempted to convince them that they must try to find General Custer and deliver a message. The Major would not order a trooper out for he felt it would mean certain death for any soldier he sent. But a scout with the special talents the Indian had for moving silently and unseen through difficult places would stand a good chance of getting through. Major Reno later reported that they talked

In the Valley of the Little Big Horn

plenty about it, but, in the end, each refused the dangerous mission.

Pickets were sent out in front of the line to stand in the lonely darkness and give the alarm, perhaps with their last breath, should the hostiles silently creep to the attack under the blinding shroud of night. Trumpeter Martin, who had stayed with Benteen's Battalion after delivering Custer's message, was instructed to sound reveille at 2 A.M. to rouse any who may have fallen into the drugged sleep of the completely fatigued, for with the dawn would come those dancing demons in the valley. With the first show of light in the eastern sky, about 2:30 or 3 o'clock on the morning of June 26th, 1876, two shots were fired on the slope of Reno's bluff as a signal for the Sioux to start a new day of furious attempts to wipe out what remained of the 7th Cavalry.

Custer and his five troops were wiped out on the 25" of June. Remember, - General Terry's instructions, - top of page 22, - bottom of page 23 - not to enter the valley of the Little Big Horn before the 26", by which time the slower moving infantry would be within possible supporting distance, but Custer was determined to reap all the glory himself.

The following may be a very uncharitable thought. I have never heard it expressed by anyone else nor have I ever expressed it to anyone before this, but I have often wondered if Custer did not send Reno, Benteen and McDougall, amongst his best Indian fighters, off on "wild goose-chases," but keeping his close relatives with him that they might reap some reflected glory? However, that would seem to indicate a plan and I can find no indication of his having had one, nor did his subordinates seem to know of any.

May I be forgiven if I am wrong! Edward M. Offley.

See page 24.

CHAPTER 5

Stand of the Combined Command

THE MORNING of the 26th dawned overcast and rainy. As the faint light grew stronger, the firing increased from a sporadic sputtering, like the approach of a heavy storm, to a full downpour of lead, until it raked the hill like wind-driven hail. Major Reno stated that on the morning of the 26th they experienced the heaviest fire of his entire Army career, which included much action during the Civil War. The Sioux, fresh from their victory over General Custer and his men, returned with a spirit to finish the job they had so ably started on Major Reno and his command the day before. Now, not only were the hostiles pecking at them with their Winchesters, but the troopers were being nailed by their own stingers, as the Springfields taken from Custer's dead troopers were brought into the fight.

The Indians had excellent cover and when a trooper got a chance to take a shot, the only target he could find would be the smoke puffs from the hostiles' guns. The Indians would lay down such a heavy fire that a soldier could not risk showing himself to shoot back. Then the hostiles would charge up the bluff This was repeated over and over again during the morning of the 26th. Although the fighting was as fierce as the day before, as a result of the defenses the men were able to lay during the night, casualties were much lighter. There were 900 to 1000 braves firing on the battalion at one time, with two or three times more that number waiting for a chance to

45-70 shells found by Mr. and Mrs. John S. duMont, 1954, on Reno's Bluff, Valley of the Little Big Horn.

get close enough to shoot. They would come into range in small parties and join the fight. When a group withdrew to replenish ammunition, a new group would take its place. Captain Benteen stated that on the morning of the 26th, "They had little picnic parties of a regiment or two standing around in the bottom looking on. There was no place to put them. I

Stand of the Combined Command

think there were a couple thousand around us, waiting for a place to shoot from."

Between nine and ten o'clock the battalion was subjected to what proved to be the last all-out attempt to overwhelm them. The Indians mounted several fierce charges, hitting the positions held by D, H, and M Companies the hardest. The Sioux worked themselves so close to H Company that they threw dirt, stones, lances and arrows at them by hand. One young buck even dared to touch a dead trooper's body on the firing line with a coup stick. These warriors of the plains often considered war a game more than a deadly business. An open hand slap on the face of an armed living foe, or a touch with a harmless coup stick on the body of the enemy, dead or alive, was more highly honored and praised than a killing shot from near or far. The troops fired on the attacking Sioux from as long a range as 800 yards, and more than a few were killed as close as 15 or 20 yards from Captain Benteen's position. H Company had failed in their efforts to erect sufficient defenses during the night, partially due to the fact that there were but three spades in the whole battalion and they were in constant demand and use throughout the night. The Captain was, from what I have found in the records, about the only man on the hilltop on the night of the 25th who believed that when the Indians withdrew at dark on the first day, they were through for good and would not return. He did not, at that time, expend every effort to fortify his position. As a result, the Sioux, who were quick to locate and exploit a foes' weak point, struck his position hard, and he found it necessary in the glaring light of day to rally the failing spirits of his men and lay breastworks and redoubts under the Indian fire. Again, pack saddles, boxes, dead mounts, mules and any other movable object they could get their hands on were piled on the line to give the men cover to fight from. A rock-strewn ravine ran from near the river up the bluff to the vicinity of Benteen's position, and the Indians found this an excellent avenue of attack. Finally, after raising some defense works, H Company was able to drive off those hostiles who had gotten close enough to cause havoc amidst the command with a cross fire. The Indians shifted their point of attack to one side. Standing upright in apparent contempt and disregard for the bullets that buzzed his ears, Benteen told Reno that he had just driven these hostiles from in front of his position, and suggested that Major Reno lead a charge to push them back. Reno agreed. Captain Benteen, still standing miraculously unscratched in the midst of a hail of lead, gave the command to start the charge. He bellowed above the roar of battle, "All right, ready, boys,—now charge and give them hell!" Standing firm, where he was, he watched Major Reno lead the assault that ended the last serious threat of complete annihilation for the 7th Regiment. After being driven off by Reno's charge, the Indians stayed back, and although they still laid down a heavy fire, they no longer threatened to breach Reno's defenses.

About noon it was obvious that the rate of fire from the Sioux was decreasing, and the Indians could be seen leaving the bluffs and returning to the village in groups. Many arrows were used in the last few assaults and it was therefore supposed that they were returning to the village for more ammunition. When it was apparent that the Sioux had left only chosen sharpshooters to hold the troops down and would not again attack in force, it was thought that General Custer was finally returning with support.

Now that the deafening roar of battle had left the air and allowed it to carry other sounds, the pitiful cry for water of the half hundred wounded could be heard. The last opportunity the troops had to fill canteens was 24 hours earlier while fording the Little Big Horn, and all throats were parched from the heat of combat and most water containers were dry. The men who had not felt their bodies torn by hot lead could wait, but those who had spilled their blood on the dry ground and lay with the fires of fever searing their bodies could wait no longer. Some of the bravest men in the history of our country, after coming through the near-certain death, volunteered to

Stand of the Combined Command

make an attempt to get water for their suffering comrades. Now that most of the Indians had withdrawn, these men knew that all that remained for them to do in order to come through this ordeal alive was to lay behind the defenses and await res-

Mouth of the water carrier ravine where the valiant troopers of the water detail, while securing water for the wounded, exposed themselves to hostile fire from Indians hidden among the trees across the river.

cue by the forces moving in their direction. Instead, they offered to place their lives on the line, and move down from the comparative safety of the bluff top, exposing themselves to the deadly fire of Indian snipers, to get water for the wounded. Canteens and camp kettles were collected. Under deadly peril of their lives, the water detail brought relief to the suffering men, but not without a price paid in their own blood. Though no trooper was killed in the several journeys made that after-

In the Valley of the Little Big Horn

noon, the prone ranks of the wounded were increased by the number of at least three.

The action of the water detail had no bearing on the subject that the Court was investigating and consequently was not examined during its sessions. An exciting account of their heroic action may be found in Mr. E. A. Brininstool's book, "Troopers with Custer." This book was first published in 1925 in a smaller edition under the title of "A Trooper with Custer." Mr. Brininstool had the honor and pleasure of personally talking and corresponding with many of the men who took part in the battle. The story of Lieutenant DeRudio and Sergeant O'Neill is greatly expanded in his book, and there are accounts by others who were not called as witnesses by the Court. Though I am sure the information Mr. Brininstool presented in his work is accurate and fully documented by him, I did not feel free to use it in this writing. As I have stated, my intention is to present the story exactly as I have found it recorded in the official files of the U. S. Army as this information was taken only $2\frac{1}{2}$ years after the actual battle and was given under solemn oath.

By midafternoon, the part of the village that could be seen from the bluff began to show signs of preparations for moving. With the Sioux snipers still holding the troops down, they lay in wait for the next development. By six that evening, the whole village began to move in mass. Captain Moylan reported that it looked like an immense buffalo herd on the move, three miles long and several hundred yards wide. The departure was hasty for a village of that size, and many of the Indians' belongings were left behind. This could mean but one thing: the move was forced by the approach of General Terry's column. With hostile snipers still firing on them till dark, Major Reno could see no advantage in moving off the bluff, and so decided to remain there until morning.

After dark, Major Reno instructed trumpeter Martin to sound the bugle calls, "Recall" and "March", so that any troopers who may have been separated from the command and

70

Stand of the Combined Command

still lived might locate them by the calls, and thus find their way back to safety. The clear notes of the bugle, drifting in the night air, fell on the deaf ears of 264 dead men of the 7th Regiment. Only four of the regiment outside the command on the bluff still lived and were able to respond. Interpreter Girard and scout Billy Jackson arrived safely on Reno's bluff at about 10 P.M. At 3 A.M. on the morning of the 27th, Lieutenant DeRudio and Sergeant O'Neill finally found their way back, after two harrowing days and nights. The story of DeRudio and O'Neill follows.

On the afternoon of the 25th, after Major Reno's skirmish line was forced to withdraw into the timber, Lieutenant DeRudio, with five or six men, part of A Company under Captain Moylan, were scouting the timber on foot for infiltrating hostiles. Before they had made contact, the company trumpeter, who was the Lieutenant's orderly, brought his horse and told him the command was about to move out. The men with him immediately ran for their mounts in fear of being left behind. DeRudio attempted to calm them and keep the troopers under control, but they would pay him no heed and began to push their way by him. As the last man came up, the Lieutenant ordered him to go back and get the company guidon, which had been planted in a bank some 30 or 40 yards away. The man refused, and said it was too hot for him there. He forced his way by, and hurried after his comrades, leaving the Lieutenant standing alone. DeRudio could see no sign of Indians, so mounted his horse and trotted forward to retrieve the guidon. As he grabbed the staff of the company banner, the Sioux came at him through the woods. Swinging his mount, he bolted away at a gallop, with A Company's colors flying in the winds, pursued by a volley of shots that came close to laying him out. After dodging through the trees and getting clear of his attackers, DeRudio found that the column had left him behind. What happened to his horse at this time is not clear, as this question was not asked during the Inquiry. One account from a source other than the Inquiry Records alleges that he

71

In the Valley of the Little Big Horn

tried to follow after the battalion and had his mount shot from under him.

On the command's departure, the Indians lost interest in the woods and charged out on the plain in hot pursuit. DeRudio could do nothing but watch in horror as they cut the rear of the column to ribbons. Then his attention was caught by a column of cavalry that appeared on the far bank, a couple of miles upstream, approaching the point where Major Reno crossed to start the attack. The Indians saw the column now too, and stood poised, waiting to see if they would ford and charge the village. This was the approach of Captain Benteen's battalion that was being watched so intently. Benteen witnessed part of Major Reno's charging retreat across the plain, and when he saw Reno's men rallying on the hill after fording the river, he turned his troops about in their tracks, and rode back behind the bluffs, to go up and join them.

With Major Reno's battalion driven back across the river and badly mauled, and the new threat of attack turning about and disappearing from the scene, most of the hostiles now felt free to move down river, where sporadic gunfire could be heard. They went to join in what little was left of the Custer battle. It is probable that by the time they rode the four miles to the Custer Battlefield, the General and his whole battalion were already dead.

Lieutenant DeRudio was joined shortly by Sergeant O'Neill of G Company, who had also been dismounted the hard way in the retreat across the plain. The two men, not caring to try their luck again on the open ground, especially on foot, laid low and eventually were joined by Mr. Girard and scout Billy Jackson. Girard had not run the "gauntlet" with the troops. Having missed the head of the column, he believed that to ride out on the plain after them would be suicide, so he stayed in the timber. With him at the time was Charlie Reynolds, one of the best and most famous white scouts of his day. Both men still held their mounts and Girard thought that they might work their way out through the timber and brush that ran in

72

Stand of the Combined Command

irregular patches along the river. But Reynolds decided to make a run for it. Girard tried to dissuade him, but Charlie mounted and burst from the timber at a gallop. The Indians were on him right away and as they closed in around him he fought back until he was struck from his saddle. With one foot caught in a stirrup, his panicky horse dragged him over a rise. The last Girard saw of the tragedy was the backs of the whooping Sioux as they chased after him. After the four men found each other in the timber, and upon talking their plight over, they decided to wait for night to make their move together. They hoped that in the darkness they might slip by the Indians who had by now returned in force, find a ford, and cross the river to rejoin the command on the bluffs.

Shortly after dark, Mr. Girard and Billy Jackson, who still had their mounts, ventured out of the timber. The Lieutenant and O'Neill walked behind, holding to the horses' tails, so as not to be separated. Before they could find a crossing in the inky blackness, they blundered into a band of hostiles. It was a complete surprise to both parties. When they were challenged by a guttural voice in the night saying "How", Girard and Jackson immediately wheeled their mounts and galloped off, leaving their two companions on foot, standing alone. The Indians, having no idea of the size of the unfriendly force that had stumbled onto them, took no chances. They burst away and across the river almost as fast as Girard and Jackson had left in the opposite direction. DeRudio and O'Neill fired a few shots after the Indians to keep them moving, and hastily made their way back to the shelter of the timber.

DeRudio and O'Neill dared not move again that night, for fear of encountering another party of Sioux in the darkness.

As the sky was beginning to show the first signs of dawn, at about 2:30 or 3:00 A.M., the Lieutenant heard the sounds of horses crossing the river to the far bank. There appeared to be a good number of them, and though they seemed to be going away from the Indian village, and having no knowledge of Custer's death, he thought it might be the General and his battalion moving into position for a dawn attack on the hostiles. It had been characteristic of Custer to charge the enemy during the first gray minutes of the day, nearly always catching them by surprise. The two troopers laid in wait on the river bank, under low hanging branches. They were determined not to needlessly expose themselves to danger again, for they had had their full share of luck already, and could not rightfully expect more. The mounted men moving in the bottomland could be Sioux, in fact it was more likely than not. The horses splashed out of the river, behind the curtain of darkness, and then turned in their direction, moving slowly along until they were opposite them across the river, 30 or 40 yards away. The light was just strong enough now for DeRudio to see the column and a great wave of relief passed over him. In the dingy dawn, he could make out parts of uniforms, and even identify some of the cavalry horses. At the head of the column on a sorrel horse, he could see Captain Tom Custer in his usual buckskin jacket and white hat. With a smile on his face, the Lieutenant stepped out of the underbrush to the water's edge and called over, "Tom, send your horse across here!" The column stopped dead in its tracks, and he could feel them straining their eyes in his direction. With the foliage of the woods behind him, he was but a dark shadow against a background of shadows. DeRudio could now see an Indian near the head of the line but he reasoned this must be one of the Ree scouts that Tom Custer usually had with him. After a few seconds of motionless silence, the Lieutenant waved his arms wildly and shouted once more, "Here I am, don't you see me?" The motion was all the figures across the river needed to pick him out of the shadows. At the same instant that wild whoops burst from savage throats, DeRudio realized too late the horror of his mistake. A volley of shots mingled with the Indians' yells, while DeRudio and O'Neill threw themselves headlong into the underbrush, escaping by fractions the fingers of death that jabbed at them. Bits of bark flew off trees as the slugs careened among them, and a few leaves drifted in a zig zag

Stand of the Combined Command

course to the ground, snipped off as neatly as though by winter's frost.

This party of Sioux had been among those that had annihilated Custer and his command the day before. In the dim light of early dawn, wearing parts of the dead troopers' uniforms and riding captured cavalry horses, the Indians were easily mistaken for troops. As the hostiles resumed their interrupted advance toward Reno's battalion on the bluff, Lieutenant DeRudio and Sergeant O'Neill burrowed deeper into the brush to allow their pounding hearts time to come back down out of their throats.

After a few more very close calls during the day of the 26th, they finally managed to rejoin the command on the bluff at 3 A.M. on the morning of June 27th.

There is no doubt that on June 25th and 26th, 1876, these two lived through the most exciting and lucky days of their entire lives. How can one account for their great, good fortune? It is hard to understand why a trooper lying behind reasonably good cover amidst his comrades should take a bullet in his head and give up the ghost, while these two men should be allowed to dance along the razor-sharp teeth, in the maw of death, for 36 hours and come away unscratched. There is no logic to it, so we must call it "luck".

At first light, on the 27th, the dust column of the approaching forces of General Terry could be seen. There were no longer any Sioux in sight. Where but a short 12 hours before an encampment of nearly 10,000 Indians stood, there now lay only a few scattered piles of their belongings and some abandoned wickiups. Lieutenant Wallace, having been appointed Adjutant by Major Reno, was sent with a detail to meet and direct Generals Terry and Custer to their position. There was no doubt now in the minds of the survivors that Custer could be any place but with Terry's column. While the troopers awaited the arrival of the relief column they relaxed for the first time in nearly two days. Captain McDougall, with two men, went down the bluff and brought up the body of Lieu-

In the Valley of the Little Big Horn

tenant Hodgson. His remains were wrapped in canvas and finally buried on the top of Reno's Bluff.

General Terry had arrived at the mouth of the Little Big Horn River on the 26th as planned. While encamped there, he received a report from a Crow scout named Curley, that General Custer had been whipped. Curley had been with Custer's Battalion but had fled the field before the battle started. It is alleged that he lingered long enough, at a safe distance, to witness the outcome, then rode to find General Terry. The General could not believe the scout's report, and lived in doubt until the Custer Battlefield was found on the morning of the 27th, and the grisly truth lay before him.

When Lieutenant Wallace arrived to greet Terry, and, as everyone thought, Custer, the General told him of the disaster. It was the first anyone of Reno's command knew of the whereabouts of Custer, since he was last seen by trumpeter Martin, at about 3 P.M. on the 25th. If the story had come from a less unimpeachable source than General Terry himself, Lieutenant Wallace could not have believed what he had been told. Before the day had ended, however, there was no room left for doubt. The 7th Regiment, minus more than half of its troopers, killed or wounded, moved across the Custer battlefield in a mile-long line. With the aid of General Terry's command, they were to find, identify if possible, and bury the dead.

What happened there will never be known in detail, for there were no known survivors of Custer's battalion. The story of this fight can only be pieced together from what was found on the field, and the only reliable evidence of this lies in the testimony of the Court of Inquiry, given by the men who were there. Some were officers and, as such, trained observers. Others were simply enlisted men, come to perform a last service for friends and comrades; to lay to rest the shattered bodies of this Lost Battalion.

CHAPTER 6

Custer's Last Mile

THE STORY TOLD by trumpeter John Martin, General Custer's orderly, is both interesting and enlightening. Martin rode with Custer's Battalion on the afternoon of the 25th, and would have been among the dead on the bloody field of the Little Big Horn, if he had not been dispatched by the General with a message for Captain Benteen just prior to the battle. He was the last surviving trooper to see Custer alive, and the story he told of the half hour or so just before that fateful engagement gives us the only indication we have of what Custer may have had in mind.

On General Custer's orders, Major Reno led his battalion off at a fast trot to attack the Sioux in their village. After the departure of Reno's column, Custer had followed him for only a mile, when he stopped at a small creek to water the horses. While there, he sent his compliments to his officers, and instructed them to see to it that the horses were not allowed to drink too much, as they had ". . . a lot of traveling to do that day." Upon leaving the watering place, instead of following Major Reno's battalion and providing the promised support, Custer turned his column to the right and took it up along the bluffs, in a down stream direction. They passed within a few hundred yards of the hilltop where a short time later Major

In the Valley of the Little Big Horn

Reno and his men would take refuge from an overwhelming force of hostile Indians. After moving on about a mile or mile and a half from there, Custer's column came close by the highest point on the bluffs. Here, the General and another officer had climbed to its top from where the Sioux village could be seen. It was this point that marked the furthest advance, about an hour and a half later, of Reno's combined command in its fruitless search for Custer, and it was here that Captain Weir planted the guidon as a rally signal. What Custer saw of this end of the huge village from the high point pleased him greatly, for all looked peaceful and undisturbed. Women, children, dogs and ponies were in evidence, going about the normal occupation of work and play as on any other day. Custer believed most of the braves to be in the tepees, talking or sleeping. The events that followed shortly proved him tragically wrong in this assumption. Though Major Reno's skirmish line was out at the time, and the engagement was becoming heavy, it is impossible to know whether Custer saw or heard the fight in the valley, two miles to the south. Conditions looked perfect to him and he believed he would take the Indians by surprise and break up the village, as he had done on other occasions. It was here, while Custer stood on the high point, that Private Davren, on Reno's skirmish line, saw the General wave his hat in the air and cheer. Davren was under the impression that the General was cheering Reno's Battalion on, which was not at all the case, for at that time, Custer had shouted down to the men of his own command, "Courage boys, we will get them. The Indians are asleep in their tepees and as soon as we get through, we will go back to our stations."

Custer then came off the bluff top and rejoined his moving column. The flanks of the gray horses in the Gray Horse Company flashed in the sun. You'll remember it was a surprised Lieutenant Varnum, down on the bottom land with Reno, who saw the light colored horses pass a break in the line of bluffs so far away. As the General regained the head of the command, he instructed his Adjutant Colonel Cooke to write a dispatch to

Custer's Last Mile

The white markers indicate the places where some of the troopers of Custer's Battalion fell on their way to the low rise in the distance (arrow), site of the last stand.

This is very much the same as the ground looked during our change of station from Fort Meade, South Dakota, to Fort Yellowstone, Wyoming, when I was 1st Sergeant, Troop G, 1st Cavalry.   Edward M. Offley.   See also page 94.

In the Valley of the Little Big Horn

Captain Benteen. The Colonel opened his note book and with a stub of a pencil transformed a slip of its paper into a small page of history, as he recorded Custer's message in short, clipped phrases on its face. "Benteen, come on, big village, be quick, bring packs. W. W. Cooke P.S. Bring Packs."

Adjutant Cooke handed the note to Custer's orderly, Trumpeter Martin, who was close by, saying to him, "Orderly, I want you to take this dispatch to Captain Benteen and go as fast as you can." Cooke instructed him to follow the same trail they had come up, to return promptly, and to report back to him if there was no danger. If there were Indians about, Martin was told to stay with his regular troop, H Company, which was under Captain Benteen's Command and come back with them. As trumpeter Martin urged his tired horse to a trot down the column and on along the back trail with his urgent dispatch, General George Armstrong Custer led his command on, in confidence, over the bluffs and down into the valley of the Little Big Horn, to gallop his last desperate mile into eternity.

What actually happened to General Custer and his men after Martin left the column can only be reconstructed by the evidence of the battlefield as recorded by the Court of Inquiry. Here are facts and opinions offered by officers and men who visited the Custer Battlefield on the 27th of June, 1876.

The bodies of the men of General Custer's battalion were found scattered over roughly a one-mile area, approximately two and one half to three miles from Major Reno's position on the bluff and four miles from the site of Reno's battle in the timber. This type of land was known to the cavalry of that day as "Bad Lands."

The ford, where it is judged that Custer had intended to cross the Little Big Horn and attack the Sioux, was nearer the center of the village than the point which Reno charged. It was apparent that the command never did ford the river to the same side as the Indian encampment. The first dead body to be found was on the right side of the river near the intended ford.

Custer's Last Mile

The battle had spread from there, over a large area, in a down stream direction. From the position of the dead, the engagement was believed to have been at best a desperate running fight. It has been compared to Reno's charge from the timber. But unlike Reno, Custer never reached a good defensive position and the command was annihilated, cut up and wiped out, piece by piece. It was Captain Benteen's adamant opinion that the Custer battle was "A rout, a panic, till the last man was killed."

It is an undisputed fact that General Custer never had time to form a unified defense. The command was no doubt surprised by an overwhelming force of hostiles before it could ford the river and start its charge. Having no position of defensible merit at hand, the only alternative Custer had was to attempt to outrun the attacking horde. Unfortunately, the troopers straddled already exhausted horses. The Indians succeeded in breaking the column into small units and scattering them in all directions. Locations of the bodies indicated that the battalion fought, roughly, by companies, and made their stands in widely separated places.

Lieutenants Calhoun and Chittenden managed to keep a good part of "L" Company together and formed a skirmish line. The position of the dead bodies in this group showed that when they were brought to bay, they fought bravely, in good order, until the end. There were a large number of expended 45-70 shells scattered among the bodies. Twenty-eight were counted around one man, showing that they made a determined stand. Though their situation was hopeless, no man lost his nerve and broke from his place, even as their number dwindled and death approached with steady tread.

The body of Captain Keogh and a good number of his men from "I" Company were found in another place, completely separated from the remainder of "L" Company. It appeared that Captain Keogh had at first been wounded and the bodies of his Sergeants were found gathered around him in what was an apparent attempt to protect him from further harm. All of the men with the Captain were killed, and their bodies lay about where they fell.

The corpses of 28 enlisted men of "E" Company were discovered in a deep ravine. It could be plainly seen where they had entered in their running fight. On the opposite wall of the gully, the mute evidence of their frantic efforts to scramble cut told the story of their end. The clay of the bank bore the violent marks that their boots had made in the attempt to find foot-holds in the yielding earth. About halfway up, the scars of their efforts to climb out abruptly ceased, topped by the finger marks a claw-like hand had left, reaching for the lip of the ravine. Captain Benteen was of the opinion that some of these men may have been wounded and helpless, and had been seeking shelter in the gully. Many of them had been killed with clubs and stones. The remainder of the bodies were found singly and in small groups scattered about the field.

About one mile from the place where the first body was found near the ford lay the tragic end of Custer's last mile. In a rough circle on a small rise behind the carcasses of some of their own horses sprawled General Custer, his brothers, Captain Tom and young Boston Custer, his nephew Arthur Reed, Mark Kellogg and 35 or 40 other men, including all of the balance of the command's officers with the exceptions of Lieutenants Porter and Harrington and Dr. Lord, whose bodies were never found. Of the fourteen officers and two doctors killed in the entire engagement, three were killed in Reno's command, Reno's Adjutant Lieutenant Hodgson, B Company, Captain McIntosh of G Company, and Dr. DeWolf, Acting Assistant Surgeon. There were twelve officers and one Assistant Surgeon in Custer's Battalion. Three officers died with their men. The bodies of two officers and one doctor were never found and they were presumed dead. Seven officers including Custer, about thirty enlisted men, and 3 civilians, died in the circle of death known as Custer's Last Stand.

Spread about the battlefield in much the same manner as the bodies of the men were the carcasses of seventy cavalry

Custer's Last Mile

horses. The severely-wounded horse of Captain Keogh, known as Commanche, has been referred to as the sole survivor of the

When found, Commanche had seven bullet wounds but survived and lived for several years later. He had his own box-stall and a soldier detailed to take care of him.

Reburial—1878, Custer's Last Stand area

Note the bones of a horse, — no doubt picked clean by coyotes.

Custer command. This may be technically true, as he was the only living thing from that battalion to come back into the hands of the Regiment. But well over 120 of the horses ridden by Custer's men were not killed but were taken by the Sioux and undoubtedly lived to serve the Indians for many years to come.

RENO'S GUILT, PRO AND CON

On January 13, 1879, a Court of Inquiry convened in Chicago, Illinois. It had been called by the order of the President of the United States in response to the urgent request of Major Marcus A. Reno. The Major had suffered for two and a half years under the attacks of critics who held him responsible, through cowardice, for the death of General Custer and his men during the battle of the Little Big Horn.

The Court was convened to examine witnesses concerning the engagement, particularly in regard to the conduct of Major Reno during that time. The complaint made against him was cowardice. In general, the aspects of the battle closely investigated were: 1) His failure to complete his charge on the village. Also the eventual withdrawal from the timber, which allegedly left the vast horde of hostiles free to mass in resistance to Custer's attack and overwhelm him and his battalion. 2) Incompetence, in that Reno failed to execute a maximum effort to go to the aid of Custer, promptly and regardless of obstacles.

A third issue arose during the testimony in regard to Major Reno's alleged drunkenness on the night of June 25, 1876. It was introduced by a civilian packer named B. F. Churchill, and corroborated by another packer named John Frelt. Both claimed they had been accosted by Major Reno early in the evening of the 25th, while the command was in position on the bluff. Frelt alleged that Reno was staggering drunk at the time, that Reno struck at and threatened to shoot him for no apparent reason. Every witness questioned who would have had knowledge of Reno's sobriety on that night testified that at no time did they observe Reno acting under the influence of alcohol. Captain Benteen was in personal contact with Reno almost continuously through the night of the 25th and stated that he had no reason to believe Major Reno even had possession of any liquor. If he had, the Captain stated, he would have asked him for a drink for himself. Not having the support of any witnesses, other than Churchill and Frelt, the charge of drunkenness was not taken with any degree of credibility.

The question of cowardice was far more complicated to examine. The decision and motives for the action of Major Reno were woven into the fabric of the engagement and had to be traced as a single thread through a bolt of cloth. The first act to be dissected was the abortion of Reno's charge in favor of a skirmish line before any serious casualties were suffered. The Major's critics claimed this to be a cowardly act.

Reno supporters are of the opinion that the testimony of several witnesses, including Reno himself, indicates the premature end of the charge and the deployment of the skirmish line were a result of Major Reno's keen eye, and the sixth sense a seasoned Indian fighter had to develop early to stay alive. Reno stated that by the odd actions of the Indians he could see that his command was being drawn into a trap and that "If we continued to charge, most of the saddles would have been emptied and most of the horses killed." After the battalion went on the skirmish line, this trap that Reno sensed rather than saw was obvious to even a raw recruit. Lieutenant DeRudio testified, "I saw that we would have been butchered if we had gone 500 yards further." Reno's supporters insist that rather than cowardice, it is obvious that Reno's action in terminating a pre-doomed charge that could result in nothing more than the annihilation of his men showed good judgment and conscientious leadership.

The withdrawal from the timber is another point of controversy. It had been said by some to be an indication of personal fear and the two opposing commands of "Dismount" and "Mount" and his hasty departure from the clearing in the timber were said to have been proof of Reno's panic-stricken condition. Dr. Porter was the only witness to express any agreement with this view. Supporters point out that later in the testimony, the doctor admitted having been badly frightened himself at the time. They feel that Major Reno's explanation of the situation was plausible, and that his conduct must be judged as quick thinking and fast action in a tight spot. The column had formed in the clearing within the timber. Hostiles had worked their way into the woods and had fired upon the mounted men in their exposed position. You are asked to remember that two men had been hit in rapid succession. Reno's first order to "dismount" had been given instinctively, much as you would duck when something is thrown at you. Reno then, quickly evaluating conditions pro and con and realizing his poor position, countermanded his first order with a second, to mount, and promptly led his troops out of immediate danger. The fact that he had halted the column a short distance away at the edge of the timber and had held his anxious men for ten minutes while waiting for stragglers is claimed to be proof that he had been calm and composed. If he had left the clearing in panic, he would not have stopped a short distance off and sat coolly waiting. It is their belief that a panic-stricken man could not have acted in that manner.

The second aspect of the timber controversy is full of "if's", and a main point of accusation. The accusers insisted that *if* Major Reno had stayed and fought from the timber, he would have held the major portion of the hostile force engaged. It had been claimed that the timber position, near the village, was defensible, and the Indians would not have left him there as a threat to their homes and gone in overwhelming numbers to attack Custer. The critics of Major Reno insist that this is what General Custer had in mind, notwithstanding the fact that Custer did not tell his second in command of this alleged plan that would require cooperation and careful timing by three separate units.

Major Reno agreed with his accusers that the timber position was defensible, but only *if* he had had at least 600 troopers. But his command consisted of merely 112 men and would have been destroyed at will by the hostile force that faced them. The support that Custer had said he would lend had not come, though Reno had sent two messages to him during the charge, advising that they were about to make contact with an unexpectedly heavy force of Indians. At this point, Reno felt that Custer would not be coming to his aid and that the General had foolishly gone off and left them to make an attack of his own. Reno's opinion of Custer's military skill was not very high, as he stated to the Court, "I had known General Custer for a long time and I had no confidence in his ability as a soldier. I had known him all through the war." The Major felt that had they remained in the timber, they would have accomplished nothing but the senseless slaughter of his command. He had surveyed the position and later said, "I saw I could not stay there, unless I stayed forever." His accusers insisted that *if* he had stayed, Captain Benteen's battalion would have come to his aid. It is a fact that Benteen arrived at Reno's ford while Reno's column was charging across the plain, and it would seem possible that had Reno stayed in the timber, Benteen would have joined him. But this is said to be hind-sight. When Reno had made his decision to move, he had no idea where Benteen's battalion was, nor had he been advised of any plans Custer may have had. The general feeling in the timber was that Custer had put them in a bad spot and had then run off and left them to their fate. Benteen stated during the Inquiry that he would not have joined Reno's command if they had remained in the timber without first securing the pack train. It had been his opinion that even had they succeeded in getting through to the wooded position, they would have been wiped out. Captain Benteen believed that Major Reno had done the only sensible thing. Lieutenant Hare's opinion was that he had thought Benteen's column could have made it through the surrounding Indians, but he did not believe that Captain McDougall, burdened with the ammunition and supply laden pack mules, could have come through alive. Captain Benteen had supported Major Reno further when he stated he had thought General Custer had no plan of action and no knowledge of the lay of the land when he had sent him on his "wild goose" scouting mission, hunting for a valley. Benteen said, "If I had kept going until I

In the Valley of the Little Big Horn

reached the first valley, as instructed, I would have been 25 miles away and of no possible use as a supporting force to either Custer or Reno." General Custer had given him no information on the action the rest of the command would take after he separated, and Benteen had no idea that Custer had split the balance of the regiment between himself and Reno until he had joined the Major on top of the bluff. Supporters insist that *if* Major Reno and Captain Benteen had done anything other than what had been done on their own initiative, it would have only magnified the disaster and accomplished nothing else.

The third point of controversy was brought on by the fact that Major Reno had held the combined command of his and Captain Benteen's battalion on top of the bluff for approximately one hour before moving in the direction Custer was known to have gone. Also, that once he had started, he did not continue, regardless of hostile resistance, but had withdrawn once again to comparative safety. Major Reno's explanation to the Court during his testimony was that the reason for delay in the attempt to re-establish contact with Custer was due to the approach of the slow-moving pack train. It had been necessary to bring it up and under the protection of the command, not only to keep it from being destroyed when it was discovered by the Indians, but it was also necessary to replenish their depleted supply of ammunition. Instructions had been sent to the pack train by the person of Lieutenant Hare in an attempt to hurry it along. After this had been done, it still required an hour to bring the last of the pack animals in. When the column did move, its progress was slow, because of the special care required to move the seven wounded men. After having moved only one mile to the highest point on the bluff and though having observed many Indians on the plain, they had seen no sign of Custer and his command. Thereafter, they had been confronted by such a huge force of hostiles that the command could not possibly have fought its way through. Reno deemed it doubtful that they could have survived had they not withdrawn to the previous position on the bluff. Supporters insist had Reno, even with the aid of a miracle, been able to fight his way through the Indians, he would have found Custer's battalion already dead. Captain Benteen believed that Custer and his men had already been annihilated by the time he received the General's message via Trumpeter Martin. Major Reno could not possibly have reached the Custer battlefield in time to be of any help, even had he gone there directly from the timber. Both engagements were in progress in rapid sequence, and in fact they must have overlapped. When Reno's command had reached Weir's hill, Lieutenant Wallace could see an exceedingly large number of Indians milling about in the area that later proved to be the Custer battlefield. This had been approximately 4:30 P.M. and the Lieutenant had seen no sign of fighting, although occasionally he had heard a shot. In view of the fact that: (One) gunfire had been heard from that direction by some of the men while taking position on Reno's bluff for the first time that day, between 3:30 and 4:00 o'clock; (Two) that all action on the Custer battlefield was over when viewed by Lieutenant Wallace at 4:30; it is estimated that the battle of Custer's "Last Desperate Mile" had lasted about one short half hour and had taken place between 3:45 and 4:15. Reno's supporters concede that all of the Indians had left the area of the action involving Major Reno's battalion at about the time they had taken position on the bluff and agree that no doubt they had gone to join in the annihilation of Custer and his battalion, which was already well under way. But by the time the Indians had covered the four miles between the two locations, they could have played but a small part in the fight. When Reno's position on the bluff came under fire again, at about six o'clock, it was from a force of hostiles considerably larger than the initial number. This, they claim, leaves little doubt that Reno and Custer had been under observation by the Indians all the way from the Rosebud. Every move that Custer made from then on was well known to the Sioux, and the Indians had baited and laid traps

In the Valley of the Little Big Horn

for both commands. Neither could have done a thing to help the other. Each battalion's survival had been the only intelligent object. Victory was out of the question even before the first shot had been fired. Six hundred troopers, even the cream of the U. S. Cavalry, stood no chance against four thousand plus determined Sioux and Cheyenne warriors, especially when the regiment had been split into four separate units. The cavalry's Indian scouts had known this when they refused Custer's order to lead the charge into the village. It's possible Major Reno had sensed this as he made his ford of the Little Big Horn, and that he was prepared to take appropriate action in the nick of time. General Custer must have finally realized it also, but much too late. The general consensus of opinion of those sympathetic to Reno's cause is that Major Reno's opinion of Custer's military ability could have had no more shocking affirmation than the story written in blood that day. And that if Major Reno had done any one of the things his armchair critics would have had him do the news headlines and our history books would have recorded the even more shocking story of the annihilation of General Custer and the entire 7th Regiment of 600 men.

OPINION OF THE COURT

"It is the conclusion of this Court, in view of all the facts in evidence, that no further proceedings are necessary in this case, and it expresses their opinion in compliance with the concluding clause of the order convening this Court."

With the preceding written opinion, the Court of Inquiry cleared the name of Major Marcus A. Reno and adjourned. Officially, the responsibility for the senseless death of 264 men of the 7th Regiment of U. S. Cavalry must rest on other shoulders. And thus, the record books were closed on the Battle of the Little Big Horn.

Custer's Last Mile

Two artists' conceptions of the Custer fight.

CHAPTER 7

The Forgotten Men of the Little Big Horn

"Killed, June 25, 1876, in action with Indians on the Little Big Horn River M.T." (Montana Territory)

THIS NOTATION, with slight appropriate variations, is to be found in the Army Records after the name of each man who perished in that action. After carefully searching through six volumes of enlistment data, containing approximately 72,000 names and covering a period of seven years from 1870 through 1877, I have compiled, I believe, the first documented list of troopers, Indian scouts, and civilians killed in the battle of the Little Big Horn. This list, which is included among the following pages, is cross-filed with microfilms of said records in my possession, making it possible for me to produce the Army Record of any man contained therein. These 264 names and their accompanying documentation were the original goal of my research.

In my quest for the identity of the Forgotten Men of the Little Big Horn, I have had the opportunity to examine at least 3 so-called accurate lists, two of which originated from official sources. All three are lacking nearly all the first names of the men, and contain many grossly misspelled last names. Not only do these lists contain the names of several troopers that the enlistment records do not substantiate, but each lacks some names of 7th Cavalry men who are identified in the enlistment records as having been killed in the action in question. The inadequate information supplied on these documents, plus the incompatible, alleged facts presented by accounts of

The low rise of ground where Custer and what remained of his battalion made a fatal but determined stand to the last man.

the battle that I have read, left me no alternative but to research the subject in the military records myself and thereby not only produce the accurate list I had sought in vain, but also find the true story of the engagement.

The account of the battle found in chapters 2-5 has been derived directly from the sworn testimony of witnesses called by the Court of Inquiry. This document is contained on 140' of 35mm film, photographed in micro dimension. There are 1267 pages of testimony and exhibit documents that require a nine-power magnifying glass to make them legible. This restricted the field of vision to approximately one half square inch. I mean it literally when I say I have examined the minutes of the Court, one half inch by one half inch, and it can

The Forgotten Men of the Little Big Horn

hardly be disputed that these sources must be considered the most dependable in existence.

The list that follows has been arranged by battalions in alphabetical order, as they were separated on the early afternoon of June 25, 1876. All of the casualties suffered by Captain Benteen's battalion and Captain McDougall's command were incurred after they had joined Major Reno on the bluff and were then under his command.

Officers have been placed at the head of their respective companies. Civilians and Indian scouts at the end of the list in the battalion to which they were attached when killed.

I can supply, upon request, additional specific information pertaining to any man listed. The records contain such particulars as place and date of enlistment, name of enlistment officer, period of enlistment, town or county, state or country, and year of birth. Also occupation prior to enlistment, color of eyes, hair, complexion, and height of men.

ALPHABETICAL LIST OF MEN KILLED AT BIG HORN

NAME	RANK	COMPANY
Major Reno's Battalion		
Hodgson, Benjamin	2nd Lt. Adj't.	
DeWolf, J. M.	Act. Ass't. Surg.	
Armstrong, John E.	Private	A
Dalious, James	Corp'l.	A
Drinan, James	Private	A
McDonnald, James	Private	A
Moodie, William	Private	A
Rollins, Richard	Private	A
Sullivan, John	Private	A
Sweetser, Thomas P.	Private	A

* Died later of wounds.

NAME	RANK	COMPANY
King, George H.*	Corp'l.	A
McIntosh, Donald	1st. Lt.	G
Botzer, Edward	Serg't.	G
Considine, Martin	Serg't.	G
Dose, Henry	Trumpeter	G
Hagemaun, Otto	Corp'l.	G
Marton, Jas.	Corp'l.	G
Moore, Andrew J.	Private	G
McGinnis, John J.	Private	G
Rapp, John	Private	G
Rogers, Benjamin F.	Private	G
Seafferman, Henry	Private	G
Selby, Crawford	Saddler	G
Stanley, Edward	Private	G
Wells, Benjamin	Farrier	G
Gordon, Henry	Private	M
Klotzbucher, Henry	Private	M
Lorentz, George	Private	M
Meyer, William D.	Private	M
O'Harra, Miles F.	Serg't.	M
Scollin, Henry M.	Corp'l.	M
Smith, George E.	Private	M
Strung, Fred	Corp'l.	M
Summers, David	Private	M
Tanner, James J.*	Private	M
Turley, Henry	Private	M
Voigt, Henry C.	Private	M
Braun, Frank*	Private	M
Dorman, Isiah	Interpreter	
Reynolds, Charles	Interpreter and scout	
Bouyer, Minton	White scout	
Bloody Knife	Indian Scout	
Bob Tail Bull	Indian Scout	
Stab	Indian Scout	

The Forgotten Men of the Little Big Horn

NAME	RANK	COMPANY
Captain Benteen's Battalion		
Charley, Vincent	Farrier	D
Goldan, Patrick	Private	D
George, William*	Private	H
Jones, Julien D.	Private	H
Lell, George	Corp'l.	H
Meador, Thomas E.	Private	H
Callahan, John J.	Corp'l.	K
Clear, Elihu F.	Private	K
Helmer, Julius	Trumpeter	K
Hughes, Robert H.	Serg't.	K
Winney, Dewitt	1st Serg't.	K
Captain McDougall's Command		
Dorn, Richard B.	Private	B
Mask, George	Private	B
Bennett, James C.*	Private	C
Cooney, David*	Private	I
Mann, Frank	Civilian Packer	
General Custer's Battalion		
Custer, George A.	Lt. Col.	Field & Staff
Cooke, W. W.	1st. Lt. Adj't.	Field & Staff
Lord, G. E.	Ass't. Surg.	Field & Staff
Sharrow, W. W.	Serg't. Maj.	NCO Staff
Voss, Henry	Chief Trump.	NCO Staff
Custer, Thomas W.	Captain	C
Harrington, H. M.	2nd Lt.	C
Allen, Fred E.	Private	C
Bobo, Edwin	1st Serg't.	C
Brightfield, John	Private	C
Bucknell, Thomas J.	Private	C
Criddle, Christopher	Private	C
Eisemann, George	Private	C

NAME	RANK	COMPANY
Engel, Gustave	Private	C
Farrand, James	Private	C
Finckle, August	Serg't.	C
Finley, Jeremiah	Serg't.	C

Major Gen. George Armstrong Custer

Foley, John	Corp'l.	C
French, Henry E.	Corp'l.	C
Griffin, Patrick	Private	C
Hathersall, James	Private	C
Howell, George	Saddler	C
King, John	Private	C
Kramer, William	Trumpeter	C
Lewis, John	Private	C
Mayer, August	Private	C
Meier, Frederick	Private	C
Phillips, Edgar	Private	C

NAME	RANK	COMPANY
Rauter, John	Private	C
Rix, Edward	Private	C
Russell, James H.	Private	C
Ryan, Daniel	Corp'l.	C
Shade, Sam L.	Private	C
Shea, Jerimiah	Private	C
Short, Nathan	Private	C
St. John, Ludwick	Private	C
Stuart, Alphense	Private	C
Stungevitz, Ygnatz	Private	C
Thadus, John	Private	C
Van Allen, Garrett	Private	C
Warner, Oscar T.	Private	C
Wright, Willis B.	Private	C
Wyman, Henry	Private	C
Smith, A. E.	1st Lt.	E
Sturgis, J.	2nd Lt.	E
Baker, William H.	Private	E
Barth, Robert	Private	E
Boyle, Owen	Private	E
Brogan, James	Private	E
Brown, George C.	Corp'l.	E
Connor, Edward	Private	E
Darres, John	Private	E
Davis, William	Private	E
Farrell, Richard	Private	E
Hagan, Thomas	Corp'l.	E
Heim, John	Private	E
Henderson, John	Private	E
Henderson, Sykes	Private	E
Hiley, John S.	Private	E
Hohmeyer, Fred	1st Serg't.	E
Huber, William	Private	E
James, William B.	Serg't.	E
Knecht, Andy	Private	E

NAME	RANK	COMPANY
Liddiard, Herod T.	Private	E
Mason, Henry S.	Corp'l.	E
Meyer, Albert H.	Corp'l.	E
Moonie, George A.	Trumpeter	E
McElroy, Thomas	Trumpeter	E
O'Connor, Patrick	Private	E
Ogden, John S.	Serg't.	E
Rees, William H.	Private	E
Rood, Edward	Private	E
Schele, Henry	Private	E
Smallwood, William	Private	E
Smith, Albert A. 2nd.	Private	E
Smith, James 1st.	Private	E
Smith, James 3rd.	Private	E
Stafford, Benjamin	Private	E
Stella, Alexander	Private	E
Torrey, William A.	Private	E
Vansant, Cornelius	Private	E
Walker, George	Private	E
Yates, G. W.	Captain	F
Reilly, W. Van W.	2nd Lt.	F
Atchison, Thomas	Private	F
Brady, William	Private	F
Brandon, Benjamin	Farrier	F
Briody, John	Corp'l.	F
Brown, Benjamin F. 1st.	Private	F
Brown, William 2nd.	Private	F
Bruce, Patrick	Private	F
Burnham, Lucien	Private	F
Carney, James	Private	F
Cather, Armanthus B.	Private	F
Coleman, Charles	Corp'l.	F
Donnelly, Timothy	Private	F
Gardner, William	Private	F
Hammon, George N.	Private	F

Capt. T. B. Weir and daughter

Capt. G. W. Yates

Lieut. W. W. Cooke

NAME	RANK	COMPANY
Kelley, Jonn	Private	F
Kenney, Michael	1st Serg't.	F
Klein, Gustav	Private	F
Kmauther, Herman	Private	F
Larock, William H.	Private	F
Leimann, Weiner L.	Private	F
Lossu, William A.	Private	F
Madsen, Criston	Private	F
Manning, James R.	Blacksmith	F
Milton, Francis E.	Private	F
Monroe, Joseph	Private	F
Nursey, Frederick	Serg't.	F
Omling, Sebastian	Private	F
Rudden, Patrick	Private	F
Saunders, Richard	Private	F
Sicfons, Francis W.	Private	F
Vickory, John	Serg't.	F
Warren, George	Private	F
Way, Thomas N.	Private	F
Wilkison, John K.	Serg't.	F
Keogh, M. W.	Captain	I
Porter, J. E.	1st Lt.	I
Bailey, Henry A.	Blacksmith	I
Barry, John	Private	I
Broadhurst, Joseph F.	Private	I
Bustard, James	Serg't.	I
Connors, Thomas	Private	I
Downing, Thomas P.	Private	I
Driscoll, Edward C.	Private	I
Gillette, David C.	Private	I
Gross, George H.	Private	I
Hetesimer, Adam	Private	I
Holcomb, Edward P.	Private	I
Horn, Marion	Private	I
Kelley, Patrick	Private	I

The Forgotten Men of the Little Big Horn

Capt. Myles W. Keogh

Lieut. H. M. Harrington

Lieut. Jas. Calhoun, Custer's brother-in-law

NAME	RANK	COMPANY
Lehmann, Fred	Private	I
Lehmann, Henry	Private	I
Lloyd, Edward W.	Private	I
Mitchell, John	Private	I
Morris, George C.	Corp'l.	I
McIthargey, Archibald	Private	I
Noshang, Jacob	Private	I
O'Bryan, John	Private	I
Parker, John	Private	I
Patton, John W.	Trumpeter	I
Pitter, Felix James	Private	I
Post, George	Private	I
Quinn, Jas.	Private	I
Reed, William	Private	I
Rossbury, John W.	Private	I
Staples, Samuel F.	Corp'l.	I
Symms, Darren L.	Private	I
Troy, James E.	Private	I
Van Bramer, Charles	Private	I
Varden, Frank E.	1st Serg't.	I
Whaley, William B.	Private	I
Wild, John	Corp'l.	I
Calhoun, James	1st Lt.	L
Crittenden, J. J.	2nd Lt.	L
Adams, George E.	Private	L
Andrews, William	Private	L
Assadely, Antony	Private	L
Babcock, Elmer	Private	L
Burke, John	Private	L
Butler, James	1st Serg't.	L
Cashan, William	Private	L
Chreer, Ami	Private	L
Crisfeld, William B.	Private	L
Duggan, John	Private	L
Dye, William	Private	L

The Forgotten Men of the Little Big Horn

Lieut. J. G. Sturgis

Lieut. William Van W. Reilly

Lieut. B. H. Hodgson

Lieut. A. E. Smith

NAME	RANK	COMPANY
Galvan, James J.	Private	L
Gilbert, William H.	Corp'l.	L
Graham, Charles	Private	L
Hamilton, Henry	Private	L
Hanggi, Louis	Private	L
Harrington, Weston	Private	L
Harrison, William C.	Corp'l.	L
Heath, William	Farrier	L
Hughes, Francis F.	Private	L
Cavanagh, Thomas G.	Private	L
Lobering, Louis	Private	L
Mahoney, Bartholomew	Private	L
Maxwell, Thomas E.	Private	L
Miller, John	Private	L
McCarthy, Charles	Private	L
McGue, Peter	Private	L
O'Connell, David J.	Private	L
Perkins, Charles	Private	L
Riebold, Cristian	Private	L
Roberts, Henry	Private	L
Rodgers, Walter B.	Private	L
Schmidt, Charles	Private	L
Scott, Charles	Private	L
Seiler, John	Corp'l.	L
Siemon, Charles	Private	L
Simensen, Brent	Private	L
Snow, Aneceir	Private	L
Tarbox, Byron	Private	L
Tessier, Edmond D.	Private	L
Tweed, Thomas L.	Private	L
Veller, Nathanial	Private	L
Walsh, Frederick	Trumpeter	L
Warren, Amos B.	Serg't.	L
Custer, Boston	Civilian	
Reed, Arthur	Civilian	

The Forgotten Men of the Little Big Horn

NAME	RANK	COMPANY
Kellogg, Mark	Correspondent "Bismarck Tribune"	

The following is a breakdown of casualties, both killed and wounded, arranged by company and commands. The number of wounded that survived the battle and eventually recovered has been added as a matter of comparative interest. The figures concerning the "wounded survived" only have been taken from an official list of questionable reliability, but the only available source for this information. Figures dealing with the "killed" and "died of wounds" are of course, accurate, as they were taken from the enlistment records. You may consider the totals concerning the "wounded survived" as close estimates.

Reno's Battalion	KILLED	SURVIVED WOUNDED
Co. A—8 Killed, 7 Wounded (1 Died of wounds 7/2/76 steamer *Far West*)	9	6
Co. G—13 Killed, 4 Wounded	13	4
Co. M—11 Killed, 11 Wounded (2 Died of wounds 6/27/76 battlefield. 10/4/76 Fort A. Lincoln)	13	9
Co. G—1 Killed Company officer 1st. Lieutenant	1	
1 Killed Battalion Adjutant 2nd Lieutenant	1	
1 Killed Acting Assistant Surgeon	1	
2 Killed White scouts	2	
1 Killed Interpreter (Negro)	1	
3 Killed Indian scouts	3	
TOTAL	44	19

Benteen's Battalion	KILLED	SURVIVED WOUNDED
Co. D—2 Killed, 1 Wounded	2	1
Co. H—3 Killed, 19 Wounded (1 Died of wounds 7/3/76 steamer *Far West*)	4	18
Co. K—5 Killed, 3 Wounded	5	3
TOTAL	11	22

McDougall's Command	KILLED	SURVIVED WOUNDED
Co. B—2 Killed, 2 Wounded	2	2

Pack Train Detail

	KILLED	SURVIVED WOUNDED
Co. C—4 Wounded (1 Died of wounds 7/5/76 steamer *Far West*)	1	3
Co. E—1 Wounded		1
Co. F—0 Killed, 0 Wounded		
Co. I—1 Wounded (1 Died of wounds 7/20/76 Fort A. Lincoln)	1	
Co. L—1 Wounded 1 Killed (Civilian packer)	1	1
TOTAL	5	7

Total Casualties of Reno, Benteen and McDougall's Commands

TOTAL	59	48

You will note that "C", "E", "F", and "L" Companies were represented on the pack train detail, under the command of Captain McDougall. This detail was composed of six or seven men from each of the twelve companies in the regiment. As a result, not all the men of "C", "E", "F", "I", and "L" Companies rode with Custer on the 25th.

The Forgotten Men of the Little Big Horn

Custer's Battalion	KILLED	SURVIVED WOUNDED
Co. C—36 Killed	36	0
Co. E—37 Killed	37	0
Co. F—34 Killed	34	0
Co. I—35 Killed	35	0
Co. L—44 Killed	44	0
3 Killed—Officer Field Staff	3	0
2 Killed—N.C.O. Field Staff	2	0
Co. C— 2 Killed—Company Officers	2	0
Co. E— 2 Killed—Company Officers	2	0
Co. F— 2 Killed—Company Officers	2	0
Co. I— 2 Killed—Company Officers	2	0
Co. L— 2 Killed—Company Officers	2	0
3 Killed—Civilians	3	0
TOTAL	204	NONE

TOTAL CASUALTIES 7TH REGIMENT
264 Killed, 48 Wounded, Survived & Recovered

COONEY AND BENNETT

The total killed in General Custer's Battalion was arrived at by adding all the men listed as killed in the five companies that made up his battalion. The Court of Inquiry transcript shows us that in addition with General Custer at the time was part of his Field Staff, consisting of his Adjutant Colonel Cooke, Assistant Surgeon Lord, Sergeant Major Sharrow, Chief Trumpeter Voss and three civilians, Boston Custer, Arthur Reed and Mark Kellogg. This is a simple process, and on the face of it, accurate. But consider, if you will, the notations found in the enlistment records:

> Private David Cooney *I Company* Died July 20 1876 of wounds at Fort Abraham Lincoln D.T.
> Private James C. Bennett *C Company* Died July 5, 1876 of wounds on board steamer *Far West*.

The steamer *Far West* was employed as a hospital ship, after the battle, to transport the wounded by river to Fort Abraham Lincoln. Bennett died during the trip and Cooney expired at the Fort. Both men had been members of companies that made up Custer's Battalion, and as we know that none of that command survived, it is evident that these two men and five more wounded who survived from "E", "F", and "L" Companies had been members of the pack detail, as shown on the list of "wounded survived".

A question that has no answer stems from this thought: If Cooney and/or Bennett had died during the battle, they would have simply been listed as killed in action. The question is: how many of the men from "C", "E", "F", "I", and "L" that were killed in action died with the pack detail on the bluff and have been counted as having been killed with Custer?

I have arrived at the Custer total using the only practical method possible. There can be no proof, pro or con, concerning this matter. If a variation exists, it most likely would not exceed two or three men and is relatively minor. Please bear in mind that this question has no effect upon the overall total killed. Every man listed was a fatal casualty without a doubt. If the point could be resolved, it would simply transfer a few men from the total of Custer's Battalion and add them to the total of McDougall's Command.

McITHARGEY AND MITCHELL

Fate seemed to shuffle the lives of the 7th Regiment troopers like a deck of cards on that June afternoon. Privates McIth-

The Forgotten Men of the Little Big Horn

argey and Mitchell were both members of "I" Company and should have been with Custer's Battalion on the 25th. But McIthargey was serving as Major Reno's Striker (body servant) and Mitchell was detached as a cook for one of the companies in the Major's command. The two men were with Reno when he crossed the Little Big Horn and began the charge. As fate would have it, McIthargey was close at hand when Reno needed a courier to take word to Custer that the Indians were in stronger force than expected. You may remember that Private Mitchell, shortly afterwards, was the second man to ride as messenger from Reno to Custer. Neither returned, and the bodies of both men were found among the dead on the Custer battlefield. Had they not been, by chance, selected for their fatal errands, they may well have survived that bloody day; but as fate would have it, they were sent, post haste, to join their comrades in the doomed Custer Battalion.

SHARROW AND VOSS

Sergeant Major Sharrow and Chief Trumpeter Voss were members of the regiment's N.C.O. Staff. These were the two troopers who carried instructions from General Custer to Captain Benteen while the Captain's command was off to the left of the main column. They each carried out their assignments and returned to the regiment, and shortly afterwards rode off with Custer's command, never to return.

MARTIN AND KNIPE

Fate was kinder to the last two couriers of that day. Sergeant Knipe had been sent by Custer shortly before his fatal encounter in the valley with instructions for the pack train. The Sergeant did not have time to return and rejoin his company and was spared the ordeal on the plain suffered by nearly all the other men of "C" Company.

Trumpeter Martin, I am sure you will recall, was the last

In the Valley of the Little Big Horn

man to see Custer alive and live to tell of it. Martin was a member of H Company, which had been separated under Captain Benteen's command. But the trumpeter rode as the General's orderly on the 25th and would have fallen in death at his side at the end of Custer's last mile had he not been dispatched with a message for Benteen. By the time Martin had delivered his dispatch, it is likely that many of the men he had so recently left were already dead.

CHARLEY AND GOLDEN

"D" Company lost only two men in the entire battle. This company had been detached as part of Captain Benteen's battalion and did not see action until it joined Major Reno on the bluff and moved on to Weir's Hill in search of General Custer. You may remember, Captain Weir had led D Company into a ravine (Medicine Tail Cooley) that ran from the top of the highest bluff down towards the river. He met a strong force of hostiles returning from the Custer battlefield and he was forced to execute a fighting withdrawal. It was at this time that Lieutenant Edgerly found, and promised aid to, a badly wounded trooper. The pressure from the Indians was too great, however, and of necessity the man was left to be engulfed by the advancing tide of hostiles. There is but one way to determine which of the two men was the unfortunate soul to be left behind. This part of the engagement took place late in the afternoon of the 25th. The records tell us that Private Patrick Golden died June 26, so it most obviously must have been Farrier Vincent Charley of "D" Company who was killed June 25, 1876.

THE STEAMER *FAR WEST*

The river steamer *Far West,* under the command of Captain Grant Marsh, had served General Terry's column as a floating base of supply on its journey from Fort Abraham Lincoln to

The Forgotten Men of the Little Big Horn

the mouth of the Big Horn River. The boat had slowly and gently worked its way up the Missouri River from Bismarck, Dakota Territory, into the waters of the Yellowstone. It was at the union of the Rosebud and Yellowstone that Generals

Dr. J. E. Porter

Terry, Gibbon and Custer met in the steamer's cabin to lay the final plans to entrap and subdue the Sioux. It was from here that General Custer and the 7th Regiment left for their rendezvous with disaster, three days later. When the smoke of battle had been carried off by the prairie winds and the dead had been laid to rest, the last few pages of the story of the Little Big Horn were written by the *Far West*. Captain Marsh had worked his boat as far up the Little Big Horn as possible after receiving word through the Indian scout named Curley that Custer had been killed and the 7th badly mauled. By early morning of June 30, fifty-three wounded troopers had been gently placed aboard the steamer and under the care of Dr. Porter. Before the boat left on its run for Fort Abraham Lincoln, General Terry is alleged to have told Marsh that every wounded man aboard . . . "was the victim of a blunder—a sad, terrible blunder."

The *Far West* left the valley of the Big Horn under a full head of steam that pinned the boiler gauges on the very edge of the red danger marks. Upon reaching the Yellowstone, on the afternoon of June 30, the steamer was forced to lay over until the third of July, when it ferried General Gibbon's column across the river. Late in the afternoon of the third, the *Far West* left for Fort Abraham Lincoln in a 900-mile race with death. They made the run in record time, 54 hours, reaching Bismarck, D.T., about eleven P.M. on July 5th.

Three men had died of their wounds since first being put aboard on June 30th, and all but two, who died later at the Fort, survived and recovered, due to the great skill of Captain Marsh and Dr. Porter.

WOUNDED WHO DIED AFTER THE BATTLE

Pvt. James Tanner	Died June 27, 1876
Cpl. George H. King	Died July 2, 1876 on Steamer *Far West*
Pvt. William George	Died July 3, 1876 on Steamer *Far West*
Pvt. James Bennett	Died July 5, 1876 on Steamer *Far West*
Pvt. David Cooney	Died July 20, 1876 Fort Abraham Lincoln
Pvt. Frank Brawn	Died Oct. 4, 1876 Fort Abraham Lincoln

These men have been included in the count, for the total figure of 264 killed.

The average height of the troopers who fought in the battle of the Little Big Horn was approximately 5'8". The youngest troopers killed were 21 years old, Henry C. Voight and

The Forgotten Men of the Little Big Horn

George A. Moonie. The oldest was 45 years old, Benjamin Brandon.

Most of the men who died there were professional soldiers with one or more five-and-a-half-year enlistments behind them. A good many were ex-farmers and laborers, serving first tours. When a man signed for his second enlistment, his occupation was noted as soldier. The enlistment records show fifty-two separate occupations previously practiced by the troopers who died at the Little Big Horn.

Artificer	Coachman	Jeweler	Salesman
Baker	Confectioner	Lithographer	Sawyer
Barber	Cook	Laborer	Shoe Cutter
Bartender	Cooper	Merchant	Shoe Maker
Blacksmith	Currier	Molder	Showman
Boatman	Engineer	Musician	Slater
Boot Maker	Farmer	Painter	Soldier
Butcher	Fireman	Plumber	Stonemason
Cabinet Maker	Gas Fitter	Porter	Tanner
Candy Maker	Grocer	Printer	Teacher
Carpenter	Gunsmith	Upholsterer	Teamster
Carriage Maker	Horse Shoer	Rail Roader	Watch Maker
Clerk	Hostler	Saddler	Weaver

The enlisted men came from all parts of the eastern half of our nation and more than 1/3 were foreign born.

U. S. ORIGIN

Pennsylvania	30	Maine	4
New York	26	New Jersey	4
Massachusetts	19	Michigan	3
Ohio	14	Missouri	3
Indiana	8	New Hampshire	2
Kentucky	6	Virginia	2
Illinois	4	Maryland	2

Rhode Island	2	Wisconsin	1
Georgia	1	Texas	1
Connecticut	1	North Carolina	1
Delaware	1	Iowa	1
Kansas	1		
		TOTAL	137

FOREIGN ORIGIN

Ireland	33	Born on the High Sea	1
Germany	29	Russia	1
England	15	Wales	1
Switzerland	5	Greece	1
Prussia	4	France	1
Canada	4	Bavaria	1
Scotland	2	Nova Scotia	1
Denmark	2		
		TOTAL	101

The large number of foreign born that were killed in the battle reflects the important role immigrants played in the laying of the foundation of our nation.

ACKNOWLEDGMENTS

Just as "no man is an island" no book is solely the work of one man. This one owes its existence in large measure to the unselfish aid of my family and close friends who devoted countless hours of their own time to search through thousands of pages of microfilmed documents and records.

To my mind, a paragraph headed Acknowledgments in no way repays those concerned for their invaluable help, but rather publicly acknowledges the debt to those whom the author owes so much.

First, and above all, to my wife Vi, for researching records, typing, correcting my poor spelling, editing, and for being the kind of wife who would do without so as to allow her man to pursue the work of his choice, regardless of dubious financial rewards. To the Prestons, Jim, Gerry and daughter Holly; Herb and Mad Meyer and my daughter Leesa and son Rick, for their encouragement and help in the eye-straining task of searching the "pages of history". To John Lukasik for providing background material and editing; to Mr. John duMont, historian, firearms collector and author, for his encouragement and for opening his files to provide the photographs used in this book, and to all those among the "too numerous to mention" who contributed in a thousand small but vital ways, I wish to express my sincere thanks.

October 1, 1975

I wish to express my most sincere appreciation to Lieutenant Colonel Willoughby N. Offley, United States Air Force, retired, who has generously given his permission to have his father's notes published here.

Illustration Credits: pages xii, 3, 51, 54, 101, 103, 105, 113—courtesy of Custer Battlefield National Monument; pages 4, 7, 14, 25, 83—courtesy of National Archives; pages 18, 66—courtesy of John S. duMont; pages 42, 46, 60, 79, 91 (top), 94—courtesy of James S. Hutchins; page 91—courtesy of Woolaroc Museum, Bartlesville, Okla.; page 98—courtesy of Eastman Kodak.